ALL
That Have
Breath

A Biblical Study of Animals in Scripture
and Their Valued Place in God's Creation

Suzanne Buerer

ISBN
978-1-962868-73-0 (Paperback)
978-1-962868-74-7 (eBook)
978-1-962868-72-3 (Hardcover)

ALL
That Have
Breath

TABLE OF CONTENTS

Introduction

Many God-respecting people have a special love for animals, as do I, including grief and longing for words of hope when a dear pet dies. It seemed to me that there was not a lot of Biblical teaching on where animals fit into God's plan.

I am an analyst by profession, so I set out to carefully read through the Bible from front to back and record references of note regarding the animals. I then looked for the themes and messages that presented themselves as I organized all of the notes. (No pre-suppositions.)

The research involved reading the Bible in its entirety in multiple English translations, including the NIV (New International Version ©), the Stone edition of the Tanach © (Hebrew Bible), and David Stern's Complete Jewish Bible ©. In addition, I used the Jewish Publication Society Tanakh © (Jewish Bible) and the Bible in Basic English. Since the purpose of this book is to focus on the Bible itself, it is not particularly a study of other writings about animals.

I organized the themes I found into seven basic categories. I saw a pattern throughout the Bible showing that creation is very caught up in the affairs of mankind, carried along with humans in the Fall, in punishments, in blessings, <u>and</u> in restoration. Regarding the last chapter, "God Saves", I felt compelled to discuss mankind's salvation along with and in contrast to God's saving and renewal of all His creation, as there is a matter of choice for humans to turn toward or away from God, while He otherwise will eliminate death, save His creation, and renew all things.

This book also includes some personal observations and discussions regarding how the subjects may apply to us today.

Scripture passages quoted are from *The Holy Bible, New International Version* (NIV, see above) unless otherwise noted. Sometimes a certain translation illustrates a point the best or the most beautifully, so I share that one (with permission when required).

God cares very much for all of His creation, including His animals. His love, salvation, and renewal extend to all who revere Him, the whole world and all that is in it! May the discussions in this book encourage you in your own reading of His Word, and may you be blessed through it.

CHAPTER 1

The Importance of Animals to God

The Bible shows repeatedly that God cares about and for the animals that He created. He blesses them, commands them, makes covenants with them, watches over them, and knows them. I'd like to point out several ways that the animals themselves are significant to God.

Blessings and Commands

Who were the ones to first receive a blessing from God in the Bible? You may be surprised to learn that it was not humans, it was animals. The first blessing in the Bible was God's blessing of the water creatures and birds, just them - humans weren't around yet!

Gen. 1:22 God blessed them and said, "Be fruitful and increase in number and fill the water in the seas, and let the birds increase on the earth."

(Note: The land animals were also to multiply and be fruitful, but this wasn't specifically mentioned in the Bible until they were coming out of the ark after the flood, and God was speaking to Noah. (*Gen. 8:17*)

God spoke *directly* to the water creatures and birds in the blessing, telling them to be fruitful and to multiply, in the waters and on the earth. It's interesting to note that perhaps for the birds God said "on the earth" instead of "in the air" because they nest and reproduce on the ground, in trees, or on rocks. Also, before the fall, the birds would not have been eating flying creatures yet - it would've only been plant foods <u>on</u> the earth.

In fact, God originally specifically gave plants as food for the birds and all the breathing land animals:

> *Gen. 1:29-30 Then God said, "…And to all the beasts of the earth and all the birds of the air and all the creatures that move on the ground - everything that has the breath of life in it - I give every green plant for food." And it was so.*

So we see that God blessed and personally commanded His animals.

Rulership and Responsibility

God originally blessed the male and female humans also and told them to rule over the animals. Right before that, He told the humans to fill the earth and subdue it:

Gen. 1:28 God blessed them and said to them, "Be fruitful and increase in number; fill the earth and subdue it. Rule over the fish of the sea and the birds of the air and over every living creature that moves on the ground."

The "subdue" was of the <u>earth</u>. That which was to be filled was also to be subdued. It does **not** specifically say for man to *subdue* animals, but it does say to *rule* them, as does this Psalm:

Psalm 8:6-9 You made him ruler over the works of Your hands; You put everything under his feet: all flocks and herds, and the beasts of the field, the birds of the air, and the fish of the sea, all that swim the paths of the seas. O LORD, our Lord, how majestic is Your name in all the earth!

Now, ruling can be done for the benefit of those ruled, or it can be done primarily for the benefit of the ruler to the detriment of the ruled. Which is the better ruler?

A good ruler cares for the health and welfare of those ruled, working toward a strong and happy community. A bad ruler oppresses those ruled and uses them and resources with little heed for their welfare. So our being commanded to rule the animals does not automatically infer that they are simply there for our use or consumption with little attention to their needs.

In fact, ruling implies responsibility. Ideally rulers should be trusted and looked up to by the ones they rule, protect the community, maintain a healthful environment, and provide guidance, justice, and possibly some direction for them. It's what good rulers do. Noah is an example of leading for the benefit of those led - he brought animals on and off the ark, for the purpose of saving them and obeying God. (*Gen. 6:19, Gen. 7:2 -3, Gen. 8:17*)

Keep in mind also that the original command for both man and woman to rule the animals was given before the fall into sin and death. This rulership originally pertained to the good creation, when killing and death were not in the picture. It was rulership over a peaceable kingdom and the Garden of Eden. It was intended as a good rulership, where Good prevailed.

In some cases later, God specifically gave rulership of both animals and people in the same breath (the same "rulership" word), such as to Nebuchadnezzar: "*You, O king, are the king of kings. The God of heaven has given you dominion and might and glory; in your hands He has placed mankind and the beasts of the field and birds of the air. Wherever they live, He has made you ruler over them all…*" (*Daniel 2:37 -38*)

One's first impulse might be to think that it would be mighty hard to rule birds of the sky, but their homes, water, and much of their food is on the earth, so man can and does have a great effect on the birds of the sky - not to mention other effects such as the hunting and domestication of birds as well, as was done then and now.

In the case of Nebuchadnezzar, he was sent a dream that depicted his rulership as a great and mighty tree: "*Its leaves were beautiful, its fruit abundant, and on it was food for all. Under it the beasts of the field found shelter, and the birds of the air lived in its branches; from it every creature was fed*". (*Daniel 4:12*) Obviously this depiction of rulership, given by God, was of benefit to all, including the animals, and not a hardship. And when the angel in the dream said, "*Cut down the tree... Let the animals flee from under it and the birds from its branches*" (*Daniel 4:14*), that showed the results of rulership removed (by God). The animals lost the <u>benefits</u> of good rulership.

The angel also said, "*Let him... share earth's verdure with the beasts. Let his mind be altered from that of a man, and let him be given the mind of a beast... so that <u>all creatures</u> may know that the Most High is sovereign over the realm of man, and He gives it to whom He wishes and He may set over it even the lowest of men.*" (*Daniel 4:12-14* (*JPS Tanakh (Jewish Bible)*)) In other words, it was to show to Nebuchadnezzar, humans, <u>and animals</u> that God (not man) has the ultimate sovereignty and gives rulership of man's kingdom and of animals as He wishes.

An example of bad rulership affecting animals is stated in Nehemiah: "*On account of our sins (the land) yields its abundant crops to kings whom You have set over us. They rule over our bodies and <u>our beasts</u> as they please, and we are in great distress!*" (*Neh. 9:37* (*JPS Tanach*)) - operative words here being "as they please" - the benefit is going mainly to the kings, not to the people and animals.

In fact, Man's original responsibility was to cultivate and care for the Garden of Eden - mankind, <u>the ruler</u>, was to <u>take care of it</u>:

> Gen. 2:15 The LORD God took the man and put him in the Garden of Eden to work it and <u>take care of it</u>.

So man's rulership of the animals does not mean that they exist solely for man's use and consumption - man is responsible to some degree for their care and livelihood.

The Importance of Animal Relationships with Man

God wanted to provide Adam with a helper, and the <u>animals</u> were initially presented to Adam as potential associates. (*Gen. 2:18, Gen. 2:20*) It would seem that candidates even being considered as helpmates for the man were at a respectable enough level that they were not simply creatures made only for the use of man, as some claim. And although the animals were not found suitable as helpmates who would totally assuage Adam's aloneness, there have been relationships between man and animals, such as a man and his dog, his horse, or his oxen, that are quite close and successful for working <u>together</u> to accomplish a task.

Another reason God brought the animals to Adam was to see what he would call them. All beasts and birds were given names by Adam. The Bible says the man assigned names to "all" the cattle and to the birds of the sky and to "every" beast of the field. So it may even be possible that he was not just naming species or kinds, but personally naming each individual animal.

Names are important in the Bible, especially the name of God. God personally or through angels specifically dictated what the names of certain important unborn people were to be. It is interesting to note that there is no report of inanimate objects being named by Adam - perhaps it wasn't worthy of mention. It is only Adam's fellow living creatures, the beasts, the birds, and his wife. And God personally brought them to be named, so it was significant. (*Gen. 2:19 -20*) By the way, God Himself named "Adam" ("man" or "mankind"). (*Gen. 5:2*)

Covenants

One might think that biblical covenants were only between God and man, but God made covenants with His animals, too.

God established a covenant with all of the <u>animals</u> that departed the ark - never again would He destroy all by flood. The rainbow is a sign to all, animals included. God established the covenant with Noah and his sons too, of course, but God repeatedly said the covenant is between Him and <u>all flesh</u> and specifically named them out:

> *Gen. 9:8-13, Gen. 9:16 Then God said to Noah and to his sons with him: "I now establish My covenant with you and with your descendants after you <u>and with every living creature that was with you- the birds, the livestock and all wild animals... every living creature on earth</u>. I establish My covenant with you: Never again will all life be cut off by the waters of a flood... This is the sign of the covenant I am making between Me and you <u>and every living creature with you, a covenant for all generations to come</u>: I have set My rainbow in the clouds, and it will be the sign of the covenant between Me and <u>the earth</u>... Whenever the rainbow appears in the clouds, I will see it and remember the everlasting covenant between God and <u>all living creatures of every kind</u> on the earth."*

A future covenant with God that includes the animals is recorded in Hosea: *"In that day I will make a covenant for them with the <u>beasts of the field and the birds of the air and the creatures that move along the ground</u>. Bow and sword and battle I will abolish from the land, so that <u>all</u> may lie down in safety."* (Hos. 2:18) The covenant of war abolishment and peace and safety is for the humans <u>and</u> animals, that none will harm another.

It possibly relates to the peaceable kingdom written of by Isaiah, where humans <u>and animals</u> will know God and live in a truly good, God-honoring way:

> *Isa. 11:6-9 The wolf will live with the lamb, the leopard will lie down with the goat, the calf and the lion and the yearling together; and a little child will*

lead them. The cow will feed with the bear, their young will lie down together, and the lion will eat straw like the ox. The infant will play near the hole of the cobra, and the young child put his hand into the viper's nest. They will neither harm nor destroy on all My holy mountain, for <u>the earth</u> will be full of the knowledge of the LORD as the waters cover the sea.

That last verse clarifies that the <u>animals</u> will neither harm nor destroy, because they, as part of the earth, will be full of the knowledge of the Lord - <u>abundantly</u> full of it, as the waters cover the sea! If you have ever seen the sea, you know this is a very large expanse. The animals will be abundantly *filled* with the knowledge of the Lord and behave accordingly, as God wishes them to do. The above scripture specifically says animals will do this and gives several examples of them doing so.

There are some who say that only man can have knowledge and obey God's law. But clearly the above passages show that animals can and will be full of the knowledge of God, obeying His law of love themselves.

Endowments and Gifts

God created the animals according to their kinds, with differences between them, all of which were good:

Gen. 1:25 God made the wild animals according to their kinds, the livestock according to their kinds, and all the creatures that move along the ground according to their kinds. And God saw that it was good.

We can observe that He gave remarkably good gifts to the animals, which He did not give to humans. On the animals He bestowed gifts especially for them.

Consider how God gave the ability to fly to birds, bats, and insects (not humans). Think of it - to the "lowly" bug, He gave the dance of flight! How mankind has wished for that one!

Most animals received sharper senses of smell and hearing by far than what humans have. Sometimes we humans, based on our own experience, forget that or don't understand. A human walking a dog with a leash often has no patience when the dog stops to sniff something - for crying out loud, what could be so fascinating about the base of that tree? The human drags the dog on. But to the dog it was something fascinating to read. Conversely, a dog just doesn't understand why a human sits motionless, staring at a book. Good grief, what is so fascinating about a hunk of paper to warrant that kind of attention? Way to waste the day! He's not even sniffing it, for heaven's sake! But to the human, it is fascinating to read. We each have our own gifts and skills.

Animals were given beautiful silky -soft and/or thick fur, bright-feathered, warm plumage, or iridescent, colorful scales - we are mostly naked. Eagles were given very keen eyesight, and bees were given the ability to see phosphorescence. Large animals were given great physical power and strength. Many animals can run much faster and jump much farther than we can. Some animals sense oncoming earthquakes or storms. The spider is an incredible architect, being able to gauge distances, plan, and discern where to anchor and build her web - sometimes the anchor points are a real architectural marvel!

The list goes on and on. Humans are not the only ones of significance with wonderful gifts such as our brains and opposable thumbs - God gave significant gifts to His other creatures too, especially for them, in their own right, and not for us.

God originally gave the breathing animals the gift of every kind of "green plant" as food. The humans were also originally given for food every seed-bearing plant and every tree with seed-bearing fruit (grain, fruit), with the exception of the Tree of Knowledge of Good and Evil. (Theoretically the animals were not to eat of that tree either!) Before the Fall and its introduction of death, food was essentially plant-based. (*Gen. 1:29-30*)

Even after the Fall, dogs and cats eat grass still. Dogs of mine have loved peas, corn, brussels sprouts, broccoli, and spinach. One of my cats likes oatmeal with blueberries and also meatless fennel/lentil stew. (My dogs absolutely adore that stew!) And in the peaceable time to come, animals will eat plant foods and not meat again, as originally designed. (Peaceable kingdom - lions eating straw, no harming/killing, etc.)

In fact, animals were not given by God as food to humans until <u>after</u> the flood. However, they were at times used as offerings to God prior to the flood. The earliest example is Abel the shepherd who brought fat portions from some of the firstborn of his flock as an offering to God. (*Gen. 4:2 -4*)

<u>After</u> the flood, when giving the animals to man as food, God also placed fear and dread of man upon all animals, birds, and fish. God told Noah and his sons:

> *Gen. 9:2-3 The fear and dread of you will fall upon all the beasts of the earth and all the birds of the air, upon every creature that moves along the ground, and upon all the fish of the sea; they are given into your hands. Everything that lives and moves will be food for you. Just as I gave you the green plants, I <u>now</u> give you everything.*

He *now* gave everything. Until this time, meat had not been designated by God as food for man, although burnt offerings already occurred. Even Noah's sacrifice of clean animals when everyone had come out of the ark was done <u>before</u> God gave the animals as food and while they did not yet fear man. (*Gen. 8:20*)

Consider this - for the 1500 or so years prior to the flood, <u>after the Fall</u>, animals presumably did not innately fear man. And when God did give animals as food for man after the flood, he gave the animals the fear of man at the same time. For whose benefit was that? The animals'! If the primary purpose of animals is to feed man, then why make them fear man? God could have left them unsuspecting and easily slaughtered! But God gave the animals the fear of man when he gave them as food, for their <u>own</u> sake.

Speaking of animal deaths serving man, one of the first things after the Fall and introduction of death was God making garments of animal skin for Adam and Eve. (*Gen. 3:21*) God Himself utilized animal product for the good of man. We know nothing about the manner in which it was obtained by God, but there are many references to the humane treatment of animals in the Bible that I am covering separately. The odd point being placed before you now is that animals weren't given as food to man yet, but their skins were given to cover man's nakedness and to provide warmth and protection when man was expelled from the Garden of Eden. Perhaps the one was needed for survival of the elements outside the Garden, while vegetables, beans, fruits, grains, and dairy were sufficient food? I think the main thing we can draw from this is that the use of dead animal products such as leather is condoned in the Bible (post-Fall). How the animals are to be treated is a separate topic in this book.

On the other side of the coin, there are a few times mentioned in the Bible when God gives humans He has slain to birds and beasts as food! I found the most explicit to be *Ezek. 39:17-20*. In that passage, God says to the animals to come to His feast table that He is preparing for them, where they will eat the flesh of mighty men and soldiers. (Understandably the main point of those verses, however, is God's punishment of those men.)

An example of future good things/gifts including animals besides mankind: It is written in Ezekiel that the streams of living water coming out from under the new Temple will have fish living and thriving in them:

> *Ezek. 47:9-10 Swarms of living creatures will live wherever the river flows. There will be large numbers of fish, because this water flows there and makes the salt water fresh; so where the river flows everything will live... Fishermen will stand along the shore... There will be places for spreading nets.*

The fish will thrive and the fishermen also. God gives life to all His living beings, and the streams of living water from the new Temple benefit the fish too. The flowing water is also for the trees along the banks of the river:

> *Ezek. 47:12 Fruit trees of all kinds will grow on both banks of the river Their leaves will not wither, nor will their fruit fail. Every month they will bear, because the water from the sanctuary flows to them. Their fruit will serve for food and their leaves for healing.*

Please note that the above reference helps clarify that God provides healing through the leaves of trees (and through many other plant sources as well). Even in the time to come He will do this.

Medicines and herbal remedies have been used throughout history, for humans and animals, and God is the source of the materials used, primarily through His plants and by His design. Those who refuse medicine, fearing faith in science instead of God, might want to consider the source - God. Some people might think that medicine is only derived from technology and science totally without God, but it's not. God provides the plants and the substances - and the healing that they are intended by Him to help facilitate. One should be aware that medicine can be a way that God Himself provides healing, and not necessarily reject it. It is a gift to thank God for.

God's Attention to His Animals

God keeps an eye on all of His animals, and He knows them all. God takes care of His own - and the animals are HIS. Scripture speaks quite clearly about this. For example, God specifically remembered the animals that were on the ark:

> *Gen. 8:1 But God remembered Noah and all the wild animals and the livestock that were with him in the ark.*

The animals on the ark would likely have multiplied during the year they were on the ark, probably resulting in more animals exiting the ark than having entered it, and God remembered them all. The Bible even says that the animals came out by their families:

Gen. 8:19 (JPS Tanakh) Every animal, every creeping thing, and every bird, everything that stirs on earth came out of the ark by <u>families</u>.

God focuses on and cares for <u>all</u> of His living creatures. It is a <u>personal</u> relationship where He knows them, and they are His:

Psalm 50:10-13 For every animal of the forest is <u>Mine</u>, and the cattle on a thousand hills. <u>I know</u> <u>every</u> bird in the mountains, and the creatures of the field are <u>Mine</u>. If I were hungry I would not tell you, for <u>the world</u> is Mine, and all that is in it. Do I eat the flesh of bulls or drink the blood of goats?

Your dog is God's. Your cat is God's. He knows them, and His eye is on them. Your dear little one is in the loving hands of God. God knows and remembers the steer that you eat and the horse that you ride. Every one of them is His, and He provides for them.

Psalm 104:14, Psalm 104:24-25, Psalm 104:27-28 He makes grass grow for the cattle... How many are Your works, O LORD! In wisdom You made them all; the earth is full of your creatures... living things both large and small... These all look to You to give them their food at the proper time. When you give it to them, they gather it up; when You open Your hand, they are satisfied with good things.

Psalm 145:9, Psalm 145:15-17, Psalm 145:19, Psalm 145:21 The LORD is good to <u>all</u>; He has compassion on <u>all</u> He has made... The eyes of <u>all</u> look to You, and *you give them their food at the proper time. You open Your hand and satisfy the desires of <u>every living thing</u>. The LORD is…loving toward <u>all</u> He has made…He fulfills the desires of those who fear Him; He hears their cry and <u>saves</u> them… Let <u>every creature</u> praise His holy name <u>for ever and ever</u>.*

Even when animals fall under the same calamity as humans, God is totally aware of how it's affecting the animals and specifically notes their suffering, not just that of humans alone. Example - this is <u>God</u> speaking:

Jer. 14:1, Jer. 14:5-6 (JPS Tanakh) The word of the LORD which came to Jeremiah concerning the droughts:… "Even the hind in the field forsakes her new-born fawn, because there is no grass. And the wild asses stand on the bare heights, snuffing the air like jackals; their eyes pine, because there is no herbage."

In the book of Job, God Himself points out that He takes care of the wilderness where there are no humans. It's not just the places where man is, but <u>all</u> His creation that matters to God, whether man is in that place or not. God says: *"Who cuts a channel for the torrents of rain, and a path for the thunderstorm, to water a land <u>where no man lives</u>, a desert with <u>no one</u> in it, to satisfy a desolate wasteland and make it sprout with grass?" (Job 38:25 -27)* Answer: God. He provides for lands where man is not there.

<u>God</u> says, *"Who let the wild donkey go free? Who untied his ropes? I gave him the wasteland as his home, the salt flats*

as his habitat. He laughs at the commotion in the town; he does not hear a driver's shout." (*Job 39:5 -7*) Answer: God. He is specifically pointing out that He deliberately chooses to free animals from man sometimes.

For God's pleasure He created all things. There are places such as deep seas, caves, dense jungles, outer space, even microorganisms, that man rarely sees or just now is discovering, which are incredibly beautiful and wondrous. Some people seem to think it a waste that such would exist if man wasn't experiencing and enjoying it, or that animals and nature's beauty were created for just man's benefit, but God made creation for <u>His</u> pleasure. The book of Hebrews says, *"God, <u>for</u> whom and through whom everything exists."* (*Hebrews 2:10*) Note the "for". God created animals for Himself and takes pleasure in them specifically, whether man is involved or not.

In fact, the creation of the animals of the sea, the air, and the land, was itself <u>good</u>, even before man was created. (*Gen. 1:21, Gen. 1:25*) Once everything was created, it was "very good" (not just good!). *"God saw <u>all</u> that he had made, and it was <u>very</u> good."* (*Gen. 1:31*) The finished creation, in its entirety, was very good, not just the humans. This is before the Fall, before any "need" for meat, the animals were THERE, and God saw that it was good.

Jesus, while teaching not to worry about the necessities of life, points out that God takes care of His animals and clothes plants in beauty:

Matt. 6:26-30 Look at the birds of the air; they do not sow or reap or store away in barns, and yet your heavenly Father feeds them. Are you not much more valuable than they? Who of you by worrying can add a single hour to his life? And why do you worry about clothes? See how the lilies of the field grow. They do not labor or spin. Yet I tell you that not even Solomon in all his splendor was dressed like one of these. If that is how God clothes the grass of the field, which is here today and tomorrow is thrown into the fire, will He not much more clothe you?

God generously and wondrously takes care of His creatures and plants, as anyone who goes out and communes with nature can see - it is beautiful of itself without the hand of man involved.

I want to point out something here about degree. Some people assume that since humans are worth more, than the birds and animals are not of worth. This is a false assumption. I am reminded of the Sesame Street © program, where it would teach, "BIG!" and show a large thing or animal. Then it would say "BIGGER!" and show something bigger. Then it would say "BIGGEST!" and show something that was biggest of the three. Now, the fact that the first was not biggest doesn't mean that it was not big. It WAS big. And so humans being more valuable than animals does not mean that animals are not valuable. In fact, they *ARE* valuable to their Creator. God knows everything that is going on within His creation and cares about <u>all</u> of it:

Luke 12:6 Are not five sparrows sold for two pennies? Yet <u>not one of them</u> is forgotten by God.

1 Cor. 8:6 Yet for us there is but one God, the Father, from Whom all things came and <u>for</u> Whom we live.

Mal. 2:10 Have we not all one Father? Did not one God create us?

CHAPTER 2

Side By Side-We're In This Together

All through the Bible, it is shown that animals are tied closely to what happens for mankind. Probably the most basic and obvious example is that when mankind caused the Fall and brought death into the world, all of creation, including the animals, fell into the cycle of death with them.

The curse carried over to the animals too. The serpent's curse was " <u>above</u> all the livestock and all the wild animals", which implies a matter of degree - the animals themselves were falling under Adam's (mankind's) curse along with the rest of creation. The curse brought death. (*Gen. 3:14 -19*)

The Fall had additional curses specific to not only the serpent but to the woman, such as woman's increased pain giving birth to children and being ruled over by her husband. I would like to note that in any case, I don't think there is an obligation to reinforce the curse - no one needs to go out of his or her way to die, or to have difficult toil to produce food, or to increase the pain of having babies, or to be ruled over by a husband. We and the animals suffer the curse when we must and alleviate it when we can.

At the time of Noah, when mankind's wickedness had made God decide to destroy mankind, the animals were included along with mankind. Because of <u>man's</u> wickedness, God decided to destroy <u>all</u> in whom was the breath of life, which included the animals - they were included in what was going on with mankind:

> *Gen. 6:5-7 The LORD saw how great <u>man's</u> wickedness on the earth had become... The LORD was grieved that He had made <u>man</u> on the earth, and His heart was filled with pain. So the LORD said, "I will wipe <u>mankind</u>, whom I have created, from the face of the earth- <u>men and animals</u>, and creatures that move along the ground, and birds of the air - for I am grieved that I have made them."*

Note how God initially said above that He would wipe out mankind, and then defined that as men and animals! He tied them together.

> *Gen. 7:21-23 Every living thing that moved on the earth perished - <u>birds, livestock, wild animals</u>, <u>all the creatures that swarm over the earth</u>, and all mankind. <u>Everything</u> on dry land that had the breath of life*

(some translations: "breath of the spirit of life") in its
nostrils died. Every living thing on the face of the earth
was wiped out; men and animals and the creatures
that move along the ground and the birds of the air
were wiped from the earth. Only Noah was left, and
those with him in the ark.

After the flood had been going on for 150 days, the Bible
says that God remembered Noah, and He remembered
the animals (as was mentioned earlier). God said in His
heart, *"Never again will I destroy all living creatures, as I*
have done." (Gen. 8:21)

Psalm 30:5 For His anger lasts only a moment; but His
favor lasts a lifetime.

Scripture shows that overall, creation is <u>carried along</u>
with what happens to mankind as a whole - the Fall
and the Salvation. Let's review some of the conditions
of original creation, the Fall, and the time to come.

Original creation (before the Fall):

- Man has a close relationship with God, going
  for a personal walk and talk with Him daily.
- There is no death in the world. (Later, *"death*
  came through a man." (1 Cor. 15:21)
- Food is provided and readily available for man
  and animals.
- Animals do not fear man.
- Pain possibly exists, because later with the curse,
  woman's childbearing pain *increases* (an increase

is a change in degree, not the introduction of something totally new). When you think about it, a productive thing about pain is that it dissuades you from allowing damage to your body.

After the Fall:

- Man is separated from God.
- Death is in the world and all creation is subject to it.
- Man must labor to get food, and animals often have to seek or hunt for their food.
- Animals fear man (after the flood).
- Pain exists and is greater than it was for human childbearing.

The time to come, thanks to redemption and salvation of the world through Jesus' sacrifice:

- Man's close relationship with God is restored: *"Now the dwelling of God is with men, and He will live with them. They will be His people, and God Himself will be with them and be their God."* (Rev. 21:3)
- Death is conquered: *"The LORD Almighty… will destroy the shroud that enfolds all peoples, the sheet that covers all nations;* ***He will swallow up death forever.*** *The Sovereign LORD will wipe away the tears from all faces…"* (Isa. 25:6-8)

- Food is more easily attainable to some degree? *"The LORD Almighty will prepare a feast of rich food for all the peoples, a banquet..." (Isa. 25:6)*
- The earth (including the animals) is full of the knowledge of the LORD, and animals no longer fear man: *"The wolf will live with the lamb, the leopard will lie down with the goat, the calf and the lion and the yearling together; and a little child will lead them... They will neither harm nor destroy..., for the earth will be full of the knowledge of the LORD..." (Isa. 11:6, Isa. 11:9)*
- There is no more pain: *"He will wipe every tear from their eyes. There will be no more...crying **or pain**, for the old order of things has passed away."* (Rev. 21:4)

Paul says, *"For as in Adam <u>all</u> die, so in Christ <u>all</u> will be made alive.... The last enemy to be destroyed is death." (1 Cor. 15:22, 1 Cor. 15:26)* Since animals were carried along with the Fall and made to die as man dies, and since Christ reverses this, bringing life and <u>destroying death</u>, the animals are surely made alive too.

Later, there will be some discussion about how after the dead are all raised, there will be the judgment of the humans that includes everlasting contempt for those condemned. (*Daniel 12:2*)

We will also be looking at references to God caring deeply for His creation, and that He will renew all things. What I'm discussing here is the way that creation is <u>carried along</u> with what happens to mankind as a whole - the Fall and the Salvation.

Later on, there will be some discussion of the individual, full acceptance of God and acknowledged dependence on Him and His salvation that are also required of humans at a personal level. The animals already know God and depend on Him, as is stated in Job and several Psalms which will be discussed later also.

Regarding the time to come, Revelation also says: "*There will be no more <u>death</u> or <u>mourning</u>..., for the old order of things has passed away.*" *He Who was seated on the throne said, "I am making <u>everything</u> new!"* (*Rev. 21:4 -5*) **Everything!**

> *Rev. 22:1-3 Then the angel showed me the river of the water of life, as clear as crystal, flowing from the throne of God and of the Lamb down the middle of the great street of the city. On each side of the river stood the tree of life, ... yielding its fruit every month. And the leaves of the tree are for the healing of the nations.* ***No longer will there be any curse.***

With the elimination of the curse and of death, and the renewal of everything, even the animals, along with humans, are restored and no longer bound by the death they previously suffered!

Rules that Apply to Both Man and Animal

God consistently mentions animals included in the fate of man, through multiple writers. It's not just one writer who has a penchant for mentioning animals. It is ALL OVER the scriptures!

The animals are often deliberately included in rules that apply to man. Some rules for the Children of Israel also apply to their animals. God at times specifically includes animals also.

For instance, God demands an accounting for the shedding of human blood from every <u>animal</u> and human being. God said to Noah and his sons:

> *Gen. 9:5-6 And for your lifeblood I will surely demand an accounting. **I will demand an accounting from every animal. And from each man, too**, I will demand an accounting for the life of his fellow man. Whoever sheds the blood of man, by man shall his blood be shed; for in the image of God has God made man.*

Note that God demands an accounting from the animal or man. And the "whoever" is referring to man <u>and</u> animal, either one (not just man). To be held accountable, one is in a position of responsibility - one is not a nothing, of no consequence. Accountability has status and meaning. The above is a case of animals being held responsible and accountable.

In another example, a bull who killed a human was to be executed in the same manner as a man would be, and the bull was <u>not</u> to be used for food:

Ex. 21:28 If a bull gores a man or a woman to death, the bull must be stoned to death, and its <u>meat must not be eaten</u>. But the owner of the bull will <u>not</u> be held responsible.

According to God, the bull was responsible for his own actions. You didn't just kill the bull because he was a danger and still get the benefit of eating the meat. The bull was killed for his own personal misdeed, and <u>only</u> for that reason.

Another case of animals being included in a death-penalty rule just like for man was this:

Ex. 19:12-13 <u>Whoever</u> touches the mountain (Mount Sinai) *shall surely be put to death… Whether man <u>or animal</u>, he shall not be permitted to live. Only when the ram's horn sounds a long blast may <u>they</u> go up to the mountain.*

The flock and the cattle were not to even graze facing Mt. Sinai when God passed before Moses:

Ex. 34:1-3 The LORD said to Moses, "Chisel out two stone tablets like the first ones, and I will write on them the words that were on the first tablets, which you broke. Be ready in the morning, and then come up on Mount Sinai. Present yourself to Me there on top of the mountain. No one is to come with you or be seen *anywhere on the mountain; <u>not even the flocks and herds may graze in front of the mountain</u>.*"

If animals are of little or no consequence, why would there have been such rules?

One of the ten commandments specifically applies to animals: *"But the seventh day is a Sabbath to the LORD your God. On it you shall not do any work, neither you, nor your son or daughter, nor your manservant or maidservant, nor your <u>animals</u>, nor the alien within your gates." (Ex. 20:10)* The <u>animals</u> are not to work on the Sabbath. They are to follow this commandment just like the humans.

Some other rules that include animals are:

When people mated with animals, the human <u>and the animal</u> were to be put to death, and their blood was "upon them". *(Lev. 20:15 -16)* Both parties in the act were considered responsible.

The firstborn animals were to be set apart as well as humans:

> *Ex. 13:1-2 The LORD said to Moses, "Consecrate to Me every firstborn male. The first offspring of every womb among the Israelites belongs to Me, whether man <u>or animal</u>."*

The animals of the Israelites were passed over during the last plague of Egypt, while the animals of the Egyptians were struck down:

Ex. 11:4-5, Ex. 11:7 This is what the LORD says: "About midnight I will go throughout Egypt. Every firstborn son in Egypt will die, from the firstborn son of Pharaoh, who sits on the throne, to the firstborn son of the slave girl, who is at her hand mill, and all the firstborn of the <u>cattle</u> as well... But among the Israelites not a dog will bark at any man <u>or animal</u>."

Animals Get What Humans Get

We are all part of God's creation together, and it is amazing how throughout the Bible, the animals are consistently and deliberately included in what befalls mankind, on purpose and specifically mentioned. If the humans are being punished, the animals specifically suffer it too. If the humans are being restored, the animals specifically are restored also. The well-being and experience of the animals seems to be directly tied to that of man. What God directs to happen to a people, He specifically directs to happen to the animals too. When nations are saved, animals are carried along with the salvation happening for their nation. It's frequently equal treatment.

There are many examples of this, and I've listed some below. Note how both man and animals are specifically mentioned together:

Plagues on man <u>and beast</u> (one was even against livestock alone, although that drastically affected the humans):

The lice (or gnat) infestation was on man <u>and animal</u>. (*Ex. 8:17*)

All the <u>livestock</u> of Egypt died, but not one animal belonging to the Israelites died. (*Ex. 9:6*)

Boils and blisters erupted on man <u>and animal</u>. (*Ex. 9:10*)

The hail struck everything that was in the field from man to <u>animal</u>. (*Ex. 9:25*)

Every firstborn died, from the firstborn of Pharaoh…to the firstborn of the maidservant…and all the firstborn <u>of livestock</u>. (*Ex. 11:5*)

When Moses brought forth water from the rock, it was specifically mentioned that it was for the animals too - God told Moses, "*Thus you shall produce water for them from the rock and provide drink for the congregation and their beasts.*" (*Num. 20:8 (JPS Tanakh)*) The miracle water was for both the humans and the animals, as specifically directed by God.

When the Israelites were coming into the land of Canaan, it was the wives, children, and <u>animals</u> who were to settle in the promised land, while the warriors were to go help their brothers. (*Josh. 1:14*)

Frequently, when God punished a nation, the animals received the same treatment as the humans.

Jer. 7:16, Jer. 7:18, Jer. 7:20 So do not pray for this people… They pour out drink offerings to other gods to provoke Me to anger… Therefore, this is what the

Sovereign LORD says: My anger and My wrath will be poured out on this place, on man and <u>beast</u>, on the trees of the field and on the fruit of the ground…

Jer. 12:12 (JPS Tanakh) For a sword of the LORD devours from one end of the land to the other; no <u>flesh</u> is safe.

Jer. 21:5-6 I Myself will fight against you with an outstretched hand and a mighty arm in anger and fury and great wrath. I will strike down those who live in this city- both men <u>and animals</u>- and they will die of a terrible plague.

Jer. 51:20-23 You [Babylonia] are My war club, My weapon for battle… with you I shatter the <u>horse</u> and rider… I shatter man and woman…old man and youth… young man and maiden… shepherd <u>and flock</u>… farmer and <u>oxen</u>…

In Ezekiel, God gave "four dreadful judgments" to punish a sinful country, and then said that all four ways would be used against Jerusalem. God specified that for each way He would "*kill its men <u>and their animals</u>* " (except for one where God was sending wild beasts as the punishment). (*Ezek. 14:12 -21)* So God deliberately included the animals when He Himself was speaking of the punishment of man, and in the above example, it was the animals associated directly with the people being punished. And you can't say, well, the animals were being killed because they had monetary value (which was being taken from the people) - the humans were ending up dead, so it was of no consequence to them that the animals were being killed. Truly, the animals were suffering the same fate and punishment as the humans.

Here are more examples, from multiple books of the Bible, to show you how prevalent the concept is - and it is God Himself repeatedly mentioning the animals as suffering His wrath along with the humans:

> *Ezek. 25:12-13 This is what the Sovereign LORD says: "Because Edom took revenge on the house of Judah and became very guilty by doing so, therefore this is what the Sovereign LORD says: I will stretch out My hand against Edom and kill its men <u>and their animals</u>."*

> *Ezek. 38:18-20 My hot anger will flare up... At that time there shall be a great earthquake... <u>The fish of the sea, the birds of the air, the beasts of the field, every creature that moves along the ground</u>, and all the people on the face of the earth will tremble at My presence.*

To Egypt: *"Therefore, this is what the Sovereign LORD says: I will bring a sword against you and kill your men <u>and their animals</u>. (Ezek. 29:8)...I will make the land of Egypt a ruin and a desolate waste... No foot of man <u>or animal</u> will pass through it; no one will live there for forty years. (Ezek. 29:10-11)... I will destroy all her <u>cattle</u> from beside abundant waters no longer to be stirred by the foot of man or muddied by the <u>hoofs of cattle</u>." (Ezek. 32:13)*

> *Zeph. 1:1-3 "I will sweep away everything from the face of the earth," declares the LORD. "I will sweep*

away both men and animals; I will sweep away the birds of the air and the fish of the sea. The wicked will have only heaps of rubble when I cut off man from the face of the earth," declares the LORD.

Zech. 14:12, Zech. 14:15 This is the plague with which the LORD will strike all the nations that fought against Jerusalem: Their flesh will rot while they are still standing on their feet, their eyes will rot in their sockets, and their tongues will rot in their mouths...A similar plague will strike the horses and mules, the camels and donkeys, and all the animals in those camps.

For the fall of Jericho, Joshua commanded that the city was to be devoted to God alone. And so Israel destroyed with the sword every living thing in it - men and women, cattle, sheep and donkeys (*Josh. 6:21*) (except for Rahab, her family, and all who belonged to her - they were spared). Material booty went to the treasury of God. (*Josh. 6:19, Josh. 6:23 -25*). So the living were all treated alike whether man or animal, rather than, say, the livestock being taken as material booty or even for a religious cause, such as to support the Levites, or to be sold for money for the treasury of God, or for offerings later. Whether they were clean animals that could be used for food besides for wool and leather, or unclean utilitarian beasts that could be used for carrying/pulling burdens and for riding, or animals that were pets, they were all treated the same as the humans, all living beings together.

In the case of the fall of Jericho, the city was devoted to God, and <u>all</u> the living beings were killed - some could say, sent to Him. There are however other cases in scripture where animals were allowed to be counted as booty, and only the humans were killed, such as in the taking of the city of Ai. (*Josh. 8:25 -27*) But Jericho was the first city to be taken, a kind of firstborn dedicated to God, if you will.

I suppose it's only fair to mention that sometimes, captured humans also were a form of booty and wealth, when taking captives was allowed. The main point here is that when humans were to be killed, frequently the animals were to be also. The animals got what the humans got.

In another case, Saul got in serious trouble when he did not obey a command to treat the animals the same as the humans when punishing the Amalekites:

> (*1 Sam. 15:1-3*) *Samuel said to Saul: "... This is what the LORD Almighty says: ... 'Now go, attack the Amalekites and totally destroy everything... Do not spare them; put to death men and women, children and infants, <u>cattle and sheep, camels and donkeys</u>.' "*

But Saul and the army spared Agag the king of the Amalekites, and the best of the sheep, cattle, fat calves, and lambs, everything that was good. But they destroyed the people and everything that was worthless and weak. (*paraphrased from 1 Sam. 15:3,1 Sam. 15:9*) Saul said he saved the best animals in order to sacrifice them to God later, but that was not supposed to be the manner of their deaths as dictated by God. These animals were supposed to have suffered the punishment of the Amalekites, been killed along with the humans, and not eaten. Saul disobeyed God, and God rejected him as king, an extremely serious consequence. (*1 Sam. 15:22 -23*)

And just like animals receive the same punishment from God as humans, they are at times mentioned as being restored along with the humans. These illustrations of punishment and restoration are primarily of physical events on the earth, but they do show a relationship in the way that God treats human and animal, where the animals' fortunes are tied to the fortunes of mankind for both punishment <u>and</u> restoration.

> *Jer. 31:27-28 "The days are coming," declares the LORD, "when I will plant the house of Israel and the house of Judah with the offspring of men <u>and of animals</u>. Just as I watched over them to uproot and tear down, and to overthrow, destroy and bring disaster, so I will watch over them to build and to plant," declares the LORD.*

> *Ezek. 36:6, Ezek. 36:8-12 Therefore prophesy concerning the land of Israel and say to the mountains and hills, to the ravines and valleys: "This is what the Sovereign LORD says:... 'But you, O mountains of Israel, will produce branches and fruit for My people Israel, for they will soon come home. I am concerned for you and will look on you with favor; you will be*

plowed and sown, and I will multiply the number of people upon you, even the whole house of Israel. The towns will be inhabited and the ruins rebuilt. I will increase the number of men and animals upon you, and they will be fruitful and become numerous... I will cause people, My people Israel, to walk upon you. They will possess you, and you will be their inheritance.'" One translation even says, *"and you will no longer be bereaved of them"*, which I think is beautiful, as it shows that the land wants to have people and animals on it, sharing in its bounty and tending it as something precious to them, an inheritance gifted by God.

Joel 2:21-23 Be not afraid, O land; be glad and rejoice. Surely the LORD has done great things. Be not afraid, O wild animals, for the open pastures are becoming green... Be glad, O people of Zion, rejoice in the LORD your God...

CHAPTER 3

Knowing and Loving God

Animals Knowing God

The animals know God. Job clearly states that they very much know about God and that He is the One Who has created everything and has authority and power over all:

Job 12:7-10 But ask the animals, and they will teach you; or the birds of the air, and they will tell you; or speak to the earth, and it will teach you, or let the fish of the sea inform you. Which of all these does not <u>know</u> that the hand of the LORD has done this?

God talks about how His animals honor and thank him, even when humans do not. In Isaiah, <u>God</u> <u>Himself</u> says:

Isa. 43:20-22 The <u>wild animals will honor Me</u>, <u>the jackals and the owls</u>, because I provide water in the *desert and streams in the wasteland, to give drink to My people, My chosen, the people I formed for Myself that they may proclaim My praise. Yet you have not called upon Me, O Jacob...*

John says in the book of Revelation that "*I heard <u>every creature</u> in heaven and on earth and under the earth and on the sea, and all that is in them, singing: 'To Him who sits on the throne and to the Lamb be praise and honor and glory and power, for ever and ever!'*" (*Rev. 5:13*) Taken as stated, that's every creature in the whole world, every human, every animal, every bird, every fish, every insect, all singing blessings and honor to God and to the Lamb! And it makes sense - why wouldn't God's whole creation praise Him? Why would God limit the glory and honor He receives to being from humans, angels, and the four living beings, but not from His other beings whom He created, He loves and cares for, who honor Him and rely on Him? <u>All</u> creation will praise Him, not just a subset. Every creature *in* the sea, *in* the sky, on the earth, in heaven, and under the earth, will sing praise to God and Jesus.

Joel says that the animals cry out to God:

Joel 1:18, Joel 1:20 (JPS Tanakh) How the beasts groan! The herds of cattle are bewildered because they have no pasture, and the flocks of sheep are dazed... The very beasts of the field <u>cry out to You</u>; for the watercourses are dried up, and fire has consumed the pastures in the wilderness.

Psalm 104 says that the lions seek their food <u>from God</u>:

> *Psalm 104:21 The lions roar for their prey and seek their food from God.*

In the book of Job, <u>God Himself</u> says, "*Who provides food for the raven when its young <u>cry out to God</u> and wander about for lack of food?*" (*Job 38:41*)

It is interesting to note that when God responds to Job, over half of His statements are focused on His animals, how awesomely He has made them, and how little man influences them - they are <u>God's</u>. (*Job chapters 39, 40, 41*) That's over <u>two</u> chapter's worth of <u>God Himself</u> talking about His animals, how wondrously He has made them, and how mankind does not control and own them all! Man is not the end -all, main purpose of everything, nor the only creature God cares about. The animals are God's, and He is hugely aware of them - they're not just incidentals made for the use of man.

There are even cases of animals being favored over the human. Balaam's donkey was allowed to see the angel, while the men present were not. God "opened" the mouth of the donkey - it doesn't say that God spoke through the donkey, but that He gave *her* the power of speech, and she spoke her own thoughts. She asked Balaam why he was beating her and pointed out how faithful she had always been, not being in the habit of refusing to move forward. She was aware of her own typically good behavior. The angel, apparently caring about the donkey, also asked Balaam why he struck her three times. (It was a good question that the donkey had asked.) The angel also said that had the donkey not turned away from him, he would've killed Balaam and let her live. (*Num. 22*)

Love and Nobility

The two greatest laws, which sum up the Law and the Prophets, are:

Love God.

Love your neighbor as yourself. (*Matt. 22:36-40*)

Animals are fully capable of love and indeed demonstrate it among their own kind, with humans, and even with other species. A bird sacrifices her life by covering her young to keep them safe during a forest fire - she could have saved herself. Elephants mourn their own dead, and I have read true accounts of cattle and horses mourning their dead. Dogs, cats, parrots, and elephants grieve their human friends' deaths. A goose whose mate was struck and killed by a car on a bridge near my house is so grief-stricken that she stands there screaming and won't leave her mate's body, even though she is in danger from cars herself.

A rare bird whose mate has been captured for a zoo gets himself captured and her freed by attacking the man who had grabbed her at roost - That bird could have saved himself. (In this account, the man sees the distressed, saved female flying above them and the captured male watching her and feels moved to release the male to join his mate high in the sky!)

A personal friend told me about a butcher coming to slaughter the family steer, and the steer trying to protect his owner from the threatening man as he himself is killed. (That friend decided to become vegetarian on the spot.) There are countless stories of dogs giving up their lives to save their humans.

This is nobility, and it is love. *"Greater love has no one than this, that he lay down his life for his friends."* (John 15:13)

Regarding loving God, we have seen scriptural references saying that the animals cry out to God and trust in Him. *Rev. 5:13* says that every creature will sing praise and honor and glory and power unto Him Who sits upon the throne and unto the Lamb.

All God's works praise the Lord: *"The LORD has established His throne in heaven, and His kingdom rules over all... Praise the LORD, all His works everywhere in His dominion."* (Psalm 103:19, Psalm 103:22)

I found no scriptures explicitly saying that the animals *love* God. But they trust and praise Him, and animals with the breath of life do demonstrate love.

1 Cor. 13:13 And now these three remain: faith, hope and love. But the greatest of these is love.

CHAPTER 4

Animal Treatment

Biblical Laws Regarding Animals

Some of the laws laid out in the Bible pertain to a compassionate treatment of animals. This is important enough to merit specific rules in the written form. For instance, it is important to honor and respect the feelings of mothers - *animal* mothers. A newborn ox, sheep, or goat who was firstborn was to be allowed to remain with his mother for seven days. Even though he was destined to be sacrificed, it was not allowed while the baby was newborn. *(Ex. 22:29)* And it wasn't just holding off on the sacrifice - the baby was to stay with his own mom. This was true for any animal to be sacrificed, not just the firstborn. Neither was it allowed to slaughter an ox, sheep, or goat and its offspring on the same day. *(Lev. 22:26-28)* That last applied to either parent and its offspring (note: the Hebrew language used the masculine form).

Another law even specifies not to cook a goat kid in its mother's milk - it is so important that it is mentioned three times in the Bible. (*Ex. 23:19, Ex. 34:26, Deut. 14:21*) So even when the mother herself might not know what you were doing (apart from her baby being gone), the act itself of cooking the kid in his mother's milk is too callous and cruel to be allowed - it hardens the heart and is forbidden. Animals are important to God, and He has commanded that they are to be treated with respect and compassion.

This level of consideration applies to birds too, including wild ones. There is a law for when a person finds a bird's nest, with the mother sitting on the young or on the eggs: "*Do not take the mother with the young. You may take the young, but be sure to let the mother go, so that it may go well with you and you may have a long life.*" (*Deut. 22:6 -7*) Admittedly this is still stressful for the mother, but at least she lives and can have offspring again. More importantly, you do not take the mother (even though she has more flesh for you to eat) and leave the young without her, which would be very cruel, as they would die of starvation, exposure to the weather, or from predation. This law even comes with a good result for the person! Not very many of the laws specifically mention a good return for doing that particular law, but this one, regarding the treatment of mother and baby birds, does.

Compassion for animals is a desirable trait for good people to have. Rebekah's offer to water the camels was part of what qualified her to be the wife of Isaac. (*Gen. 24:14*) That kindness, sensitivity, and willingness to work to help the camels (and, yes, Abraham's servant) was valued. Her act showed Abraham's servant that she was the one chosen by God in kindness to his master.

Other laws have to do with taking care of animals for your neighbor, even if you hate him or he hates you. Part of it is a responsibility to help your neighbor, but I think part of it is to help the animals themselves, to keep them from getting into trouble and to help them out of it.

> *Ex. 23:4-5 If you come across your enemy's ox or donkey wandering off, be sure to take it back to him. If you see the donkey of someone who hates you fallen down under its load, do not leave it there; be sure you help him with it.*

So even when the other person is your enemy, you are to help his animals and your enemy in these situations, partly because his <u>animal</u> needs care.

If you don't know who the lost animals belong to, you aren't to just shrug your shoulders and say, "Oh, well", doing nothing. You are to take them to your own home and keep them (safe and cared for) till the owner inquires. (*Deut. 22:1 -4*) In this passage, it applies to lost items as well, but the primary focus is on the animals which are specifically mentioned in other passages as well.

The Sabbath commandment concerns the treatment of animals and actually applies directly to them. On the Sabbath day, you are to let your work animals rest. The Sabbath is for the sake of the animals as well as for man:

> *Ex. 23:12 Six days do your work, but on the seventh day do not work, <u>so that your ox and donkey may rest</u>...*

And the Sabbath year (the seventh year), when you let the fields, vineyards, and olive groves lie fallow and rest, the law says that the poor shall eat whatever the cultivated land naturally produces without sowing or pruning, and the <u>wild animals</u> shall eat what is left. (*Ex. 23:11*) The Sabbath year produce of the land is also for the landowner, servants, residents, and <u>livestock</u> to eat. (*Lev. 25:6 -7*) The animals are specifically mentioned.

Job, regarding fair treatment of servants, said: *"Did not He Who made me in the womb make them? Did not the same One form <u>us both</u> within our mothers?" (Job 31:15)* I think this can be extended to humanely treating fellow creatures made by the God Who formed all of us too.

"Do not muzzle an ox while it is treading out the grain." (*Deut. 25:4*) This law is purely for the animal's sake. If he's doing work for you, he is to be allowed to eat some of its produce.

"A righteous man cares for the needs of his animal..." (*Prov. 12:10*) A good person who respects God and lives righteously takes care of his animals.

There are also many references to <u>God's</u> compassion and the graciousness of His compassionate nature for <u>all</u> He has made:

Psalm 145:8-9 The LORD is gracious and compassionate, slow to anger and rich in love. The LORD is good to all; He has compassion on <u>all He has made</u>.

Psalm 103:13 As a father has compassion on his children, so the LORD has compassion on those who fear Him.

Psalm 116:5-6 The LORD is gracious and righteous; our God is full of compassion. The LORD protects the simplehearted.

God has compassion for children, the weak, the simplehearted, the animals, and all that He has made.

Also consider that when Jacob gave his blessings to his sons before he died, he cursed instead of blessed Simeon and Levi, "*for they have killed men in their anger and <u>hamstrung oxen as they pleased</u>. Cursed be their anger, so fierce, and their fury, so cruel!*" (*Gen. 49:6 -7*) Curses, especially of your own sons, are not made lightly - what Simeon and Levi did to the cattle was worthy of mention as an evil thing along with what they did to the people - it carried weight and was worthy of the cursing.

Regarding the slaughter of animals, the Bible does not go into a lot of detail on the method (Jewish oral law from the time of Moses deals with it instead), but we can infer from what the Bible says about caring for animals and being of a compassionate nature, that the manner of slaughter should be humane. I'm not going to delve into Jewish oral law here except to mention that the slaughter of herd animals is to be done by quickly and deeply cutting the front of the neck, which is reputed to be an area with less pain nerves. The air and blood rush out quickly and consciousness, then life, is lost. There are accounts of people who have survived slit throats, and some have reported that there was not very much pain. Cutting the jugular also helps remove the blood, since the life of every creature is its blood and not to be eaten.

Humane slaughter avoids unnecessarily breaking bones, which devout Jews are careful to avoid. Grabbing chickens to hang them upside down by their legs, live -shackled on conveyer belts, and in the process sometimes breaking their legs while still conscious, is wrong. Sometimes the stunning that follows fails and they end up in the boiling water for defeathering while still conscious, too.

Boiling a legged, large crustacean alive (crab, lobster, crawdad, etc.), when a quick slam -breaking of their backs would've killed quickly, is heinous. When you see them in the market or on your plate in red, perfect form (not broken), they were almost surely boiled alive. These are creatures with eyes, mobility, fear responses, and social habits among their own kind. Did you know that lobsters make a high -pitched, prolonged scream

-like sound while being boiled alive? I think that legged crustaceans should not be boiled alive - it's inhumane. (Technically, the Bible says that God's people should not eat crustaceans at all, but if you do, it would be best to at least see that they were slain humanely.)

Although slaughtering should be humane, the Israelites did also hunt wild animals, an activity which is naturally at risk of being less humane due to less control in the killing. There are biblical references to eating cattle, sheep, and goats *"as if it were gazelle or deer"* (*Deut. 12:15*), so these verses infer that deer and gazelle were hunted (since they are usually wild). Also, Solomon's daily provisions included gazelle, deer, and roebucks. (*1 Kings 4:22 -23*)

And Leviticus says that the rule about draining out the blood and not eating it applies to hunted animals too:

> *Lev. 17:13 Any Israelite or any alien living among you who <u>hunts</u> any animal or bird that may be eaten must drain out the blood and cover it with earth, because the life of every creature is its blood.*

The reason I mention this is that when hunting, the method for killing is not always as controlled and careful as kosher slaughter. But hunting is mentioned in the Bible without condemnation. One can infer that the killing should still be as swift and merciful as possible, and in today's world, one can usually choose whether to participate in hunting or not in the first place.

It is noteworthy that the above verse says "any alien living among you" in the context of hunting animals that "<u>may be eaten</u>". It infers that the non -Jew living among God's people was also not to eat animals specified by God as unclean. (Pork, shellfish, etc. - see *Lev. 11*.)

As mentioned before, the concept of "clean" animals (cattle and sheep included) vs. "unclean" is clearly present by the time of Noah, prior even to animals being given by God as food for man. More clean animals were brought onto the ark (seven pairs vs. the one pair for unclean). (*Gen. 7:2*) It was because God commanded it, of course, but presumably more of the clean were needed because their kind would be used for offerings, and quite possibly because God was about to give animals (especially the clean ones) as food, once the Flood was over.

In the book of Acts, the apostles gave only a few dietary rules for believing Gentiles to initially follow, without their being required to become Jews. It then proceeded to say that the law (Moses) is read in the synagogues on every Sabbath, implying that believing Gentiles could then learn additional ways to obey, honor, and please God over time.

As Gentiles turning to God, they were initially only not to eat meat that had been strangled, or eat blood:

Acts 15:19-20 It is my judgment, therefore, that we should not make it difficult for the Gentiles who are turning to God. Instead we should write to them, telling them to abstain from… the meat of strangled animals and from blood.

The Jewish faith considers the prohibition against slaughter via strangulation to have essentially been given in Noah's time, well before there ever were Jews, clear back when God first gave the animals as food to all humans but said not to eat blood. So essentially, slaughter via strangling has never been okay for anybody to do. Although strangulation was not mentioned specifically in the books of the law, it was likely to be avoided partly because it does not get the blood out. It holds the blood in the body, and then after death, the blood starts to coagulate in the meat as the body stiffens and is much harder to drain out. Whereas with a cut artery, the heart keeps pumping at first and pumps the blood out.

Applications of Humane Treatment

I think strangulation is also an inhumane slaughtering method. It's a terrifying way to die - your body panics in a big way, and it can take a while that probably seems like forever. Hanging until dead can be strangling - anytime the body is still struggling and jerking after the moment of hanging, death was not instantaneous and the creature is strangling. When it occurs, it is very inhumane. I have read about hanging/strangling sometimes being used for slaughtering pigs, and they are sometimes even dipped in very hot 140° F water while they're hanging, sometimes before they are dead, to scald the hair off. That is horribly inhumane.

Frankly, I have to wonder even about the humaneness of hanging for human executions. It's been said that death is quick when it works right with a scaffold/drop-door hanging, but what if some of the ones where the body immediately hangs still without writhing are a case of neck/spine injury and paralysis, where you're still strangling slowly, but you can't even move while it's happening? How horrible! I don't know enough about it and certainly don't want anyone experimenting to find out. I'm just saying that even the "successful" hangings of animals or humans could potentially still involve strangling and be far worse than assumed. Hanging till dead is just not good as a slaughter method for animals, for so many reasons.

Hitting animals with your vehicle while driving and leaving them to suffer is not stewardship. Deliberately hitting them for fun is really wrong. Once I was on a double date in college with my sister, and her date, who was driving, deliberately swerved to hit an opossum crossing the road on the opposite side. He hit him, and when we peered out the back window at the possum falling over and writhing in pain, the driver gleefully said that he'd gotten him as he drove off! Well, that was one date that immediately went sour... This was a guy who above all others acted as Mr. Righteous on our Christian campus, but whom I had now discovered took pleasure in wanton killing/maiming for no other reason than sport. I was always wary of him afterwards.

Once, while walking with my husband during a rainy day, we saw an opossum that had just been hit and killed on a neighborhood street, with no driver in sight. She had been carrying her babies, and three of them had been knocked off her back. I carried the dead mother by the tail to the side of the road, then went back and picked up two babies (rat sized) in the road. The first was dead (which I set down off the road), but when I picked up the other, she slowly raised her head and looked up at me miserably. It was quite evident that she felt awful. A third baby seemed in pretty good shape and had made it to the grass by the road on his own already. I gently picked the scared little guy up and cuddled both live babies in my hands. The healthy one was holding onto my rain poncho with all his might, since he didn't have his mommy to hold onto. A neighbor came out and found three more live babies in mama's pouch. Fortunately, the woman was experienced in helping possums and was happy to take all five little ones to care for. She was a good steward of God's animals, and I bless her. The person who hit the mother and just left her with her live babies lying in the road was not.

Lab testing - Are animals like us or not? I've always found it strange when some in science say that psychological and other experiments, and cosmetic product testing on animals, are nothing to be concerned for the animals about, because they are not human and don't experience things like we do and then turn around and apply the results of their testing to humans. They use them to test physical reaction to medicines, surgeries, other kinds of biological alterations, and psychological experiments, precisely because they ARE so like us. You can't say it's okay because they're not like us and then test on them because they are like us. It's illogical.

Obviously they are like us, and concern must be shown for their well-being and comfort when using them for lab testing, as well as not wastefully expending their lives. Routine mass testing of chemical and cosmetic products to get percentages of how many die at what level of exposure is horribly wasteful. We do not need to find out just how many ounces of certain chemicals can be drunk before the animals die. People can figure out that drinking bleach or whatever is bad without needing those kinds of figures.

What is really bad is the repetition in performing these tests. Once we have the information, it should certainly do. Suffering and lives are at stake here!

A similar wasteful area is routinely and excessively using live animals for student education, from frog dissection to observing the basics of surgery. With today's technology, some of that can be shown via a video of the activity or by observation of "real" surgeries really needed or even a video of one surgery or dissection being done for educational purposes. We don't have to routinely cause suffering and/or death over and over for something that can be demonstrated via one video, especially for anatomical study. I do understand that live practice would be necessary for budding surgeons. I'm just saying that a lot of the routine use of live animals in education could be done a lot less. We should think first about whether it is important to do the hands -on at an individual level or watch an event as a group or on a video. Often the latter would do, such as in the case of frog dissections (couldn't that just be video?).

Tail docking - It's a custom that harms dogs and partly disables a major function of communication for them for no real good reason. It's barbaric and has now been outlawed in some countries. I wish it were in the United States. At the very least, the vet should use anesthesia (numb the tails) before cutting them off.

Back in the 1980's, the professional opinion seemed to be that since newly born puppies holler for the needle that delivers anesthetic, and they also holler if you just cut their tails off, the vet might as well just cut their tails off without anesthesia. Truly! Good grief - how moronic is that? Let's see, since if someone jabs you with a needle when you aren't expecting it, you scream, then that means he might as well not use the needle and just let you scream when he cuts off your finger. It's all the same, right? Um, wrong. But somehow this ill-considered logic was at times applied to tail docking, at least back then.

I've even read of this kind of poor thinking being applied to human babies getting surgery. Sometimes there's a legitimate concern about the effect of the anesthesia on premature or very ill infants, but I would surely hope that they also consider the shock to the body and heart of having surgery without pain relief. Come on! Just because they can't talk! We've got to consider how it feels as best we can.

The avoidance of anthropomorphism by the scientific community is at times too extreme. It is true that another creature's experience is bound to be somewhat different than yours due to different levels of senses, abilities, and degree of intelligence, but there are still commonalities that should not be ignored. For instance, if a voiceless creature responds to piercing with writhing, or to being boiled alive by flapping madly and emitting a high scream -like sound, it is carrying it too far to say that we can't know that there is pain, so let's just proceed with treating animals this way - there are times that common sense is applicable, and more compassion and humaneness is greatly needed.

Many attributes are common between humans and other species. Often, there are nervous systems; blood; eyes; ears; the need to breathe, to sleep, to eat, to drink, to eliminate waste; a need to associate with others; to reproduce; the fear of pain and of death... The list goes on and on. We are made very similarly.

There are even many examples of interspecies social relationships, including between one non-human species and another. Sometimes they help each other or raise their young. Dogs give their lives defending humans they love. Birds of a different species join to help other birds defend a nestling from a bird of prey or a crow. Cats take ducklings into their litter. Chimpanzees bottle-feed kittens. A goose cuddles and comforts a lost newborn puppy in her breast. Yes, there are perspectives and experiences of different species that we can't always see or know, but when animals behave in a very similar way to humans in a regard, we should at least consider similarities and not totally disallow all consideration or empathy.

The use of "it" in the English language when referring to an animal is at times a way to de-personify the animal. It drives me nuts when reading a novel or news article which has established that the animal is a stallion, or a mother, and then when the animal is referred to with a pronoun, the text says "it". Good grief! Since the sex of the creature is known, I think it would be more appropriate and less degrading to use the "he" or "she".

As long as I'm mentioning semantics, in the United States, the laws and food industry are currently heading toward labeling meat products with information on where the meat came from. Overall, this will be useful info to have, but regarding wording, I have heard that the verbiage for where the animal was slaughtered is likely to use the word "harvested" instead of "slaughtered". I see it as another case of de -personifying the animals and softening the fact that they are living creatures being killed for food. It helps people ignore the full story on what they are supporting when they buy and eat meat. At least having the information on the package thankfully calls some attention to the death of the animal (if you think about what "harvesting" really means), rather than it just being a package of yummy food like we have today that city people just enjoy without acknowledging the taking of that animal's life or considering what that animal went through.

CHAPTER 5

Animal Sacrifice and Value

The Significance of Animal Sacrifice

Biblical animal sacrifices were not to glorify death and pain or serve evil, but to serve a high purpose. There were different kinds of sacrifices, ranging from thank offerings to atonement for sins. Sacrificed animals were supposed to be killed humanely, and they were clean food animals, not other kinds of animals. When unclean animals had produced abundantly, like horses or donkeys, the Israelites still weren't to sacrifice any of them in thanks to God - it was only the clean food animals. Sacrifices were typically edible or drinkable (although certain kinds were not to be consumed except by fire, for God alone).

One thing's for sure - the Biblical sacrifice of animals was serious and important business. For atonement of sin sacrifices, the shedding of lifeblood was required. In fact, so <u>significant</u> was the life of the <u>animal</u> being paid in the place of the human, that if the sacrifice wasn't done properly, the killing was considered bloodshed and severely punished.

Slaughtering an ox, sheep, or goat <u>as a sacrifice</u> without bringing the animal to the Tabernacle was to be considered as <u>bloodshed</u> by the man who did it, and he was to be cut off from the people. (*Lev. 17:3 -4*) Part of the reason for this rule was to assure that the sacrifices weren't being made to foreign gods (*Lev. 17:5 -7*), but I also think that it was considered "bloodshed" specifically because the life of the animal, paid in place of the human's, was very significant, and the sacrifice was to be brought *"to the priest, that is, to the LORD"* and follow special regulations, not just be done by anyone. (*Lev. 17:5*) The regulations on sacrifices in Leviticus are very detailed and specific. Also, verses are just as strict about the eating of blood, and lifeblood's important purpose for atonement:

> *Lev. 17:11 For the life of a creature is in the blood, and I have given it to you to make atonement for yourselves on the altar; it is the blood that makes atonement for one's life.*

The life is in the blood, and redemption is paid with the shedding of blood.

Long before there were Jews, God instructed <u>all</u> mankind not to eat or drink blood, because of this (*Gen.*

9:4). The lifeblood of any animal is not to be eaten at any time, it is that important. Non -Jewish believers in Jesus as Messiah were instructed in Acts not to eat blood (*Acts 15:29*) - it was one of the dietary rules imposed by the apostles for the believing Gentiles (who were not being required to become Jews).

If animals were only created and meant as food for man, it would seem that the blood would be okay to eat, just like any other part of the body. If animals were only meant as fodder for humans, then their lives would not matter, as some people think. Yet they DO matter - the Bible is extremely clear that their blood is not to be eaten, because the life is in the blood, and that life has great value. You do not consume the life. You may only consume the flesh, to support your flesh, your body, which your spirit lives in. When an animal is slaughtered for you to eat, you are in essence forcing a spirit out of its body so you can feed your body with its body. Some cultures, often the native, "less civilized" ones, have been very aware of this and thanked the spirit of the animal they had just killed for food. They were very careful not to be wasteful with the body that they had taken - they used every part they could and respected the animal from whom they had taken the body.

When I used to eat meat, I was careful to see to it that I or someone ate <u>all</u> of what I had taken or been served. I think it is wrong to throw away good meat. That animal died for you. I do still eat fish and follow that rule.

I recently read a news article about a man who had raped and killed a young woman, and his crime was eligible for the death penalty. However, he got life imprisonment with no possibility of parole. I was thinking that his remaining life here was borrowed time, with the taxpayers providing his lodging and food for the duration.

It seems to me that perhaps this borrowed state of living does not justify killing animals for the condemned to eat, forcing the animals' spirits from their bodies, just to provide meat for people who in essence are dead to the community. The precious loss of life to feed them may not be warranted, especially since humans can get along just fine on a non-meat diet. A meatless diet would be far less costly to the society paying the life -in -prison food bill, too. (I suppose the prisoners might then live longer with the potentially healthier non -meat diet, though! But still - legumes and beans are way cheaper protein than meat.) Maybe knowing that you wouldn't get to eat meat in prison would be a good deterrent to doing crime!

Speaking of eating animals, one might wonder why in the wilderness the Israelites craved meat when they had lots of livestock with them when they left Egypt: *"Many other people went up with them, as well as large droves of livestock, both flocks and herds." (Ex. 12:38)* But while in the wilderness, the Israelites said, *"If only we had meat to eat!... We never see anything but this manna!" (Num. 11:4, Num. 11:6)*

There appear to be a couple of reasons why they didn't just eat their livestock. One was that the sheer number of humans would quickly deplete the herds and flocks in a matter of time. Moses at one point stated that flocks and herds, and/or all the fish in the sea, would not suffice for the 600,000 men (plus the women and children) in the wilderness. (*Num. 11:21 -22; Ex. 12:37*)

The second reason is that possibly for meat, before entering the promised land, the Israelites were maybe mainly eating clean wild animals when they could, such as deer and gazelle, and likely only eating domestic animals when there was a sacrifice at an appointed time or event (if then - there were likely too many people for all to partake in the eating of the sacrifice). They were apparently not typically eating herd and flock animals since they were craving meat.

Perhaps it had to do with their not having yet received their inheritance until they crossed the Jordan and settled in the land that God gave them. (*Deut. 12:8 -9*) After entering the land, only then were they given the okay to eat their herds and flocks - once settled in towns, they were at last given permission to slaughter and eat cattle and sheep "as if the meat were gazelle or deer" (without the cattle or sheep being a sacrifice). (*Deut. 12:15, Deut. 12:20 -22*) But while still traveling to the land, those rules perhaps did not yet apply. It is inferred that en route, only the priests could slaughter livestock, for a sacrifice or offering in God's presence, such as the firstborn of herd and flock, and then the people involved could eat the meat, "rejoicing before God", which was special and of more importance than simply eating meat to get sustenance or because it tastes good.

Moving on…

The firstborn set apart for God were an offering to God, or they were redeemed or killed. The firstborn male humans <u>and unclean animals</u> were to be redeemed, while the firstborn cattle, sheep, and goats were not to be redeemed, for they were holy. (*Num. 18:15-17*)

The redemption price for firstborn humans <u>and</u> unclean animals appears to have been five shekels of silver (*Num. 18:16*). Alternatively, Numbers says that unclean animals could be bought back at their set value, adding a fifth of the value to it. If the owner did not redeem it, the unclean animal was to be sold at set value. (*Num. 27:27*) (Presumably the money went to the LORD.)

However, certain kinds of firstborn unclean animals were to be redeemed with a (clean) lamb or else just killed:

> *Ex. 13:13 Redeem with a lamb every firstborn donkey, but if you do not redeem it, break its neck. Redeem every firstborn among your sons.*

In all cases, the firstborn (male human <u>and animal</u>) belonged to God, not the Israelite. The Israelite had to redeem (pay for) the firstborn son, or in the case of the clean animal, he was not allowed to use the animal for personal gain or to work for him - the animal was not his. He couldn't dedicate a firstborn animal to God because the animal already belonged to God, not him. (*Lev. 27:26*)

The humans were however commanded to eat the firstborn male of herd and flock, before God, in Jerusalem, each year. (*Deut. 15:19-20*) At first I thought this meant that vegetarianism was apparently not an option for observant Jews. But then I realized that it would've mainly pertained to those raising and owning cattle, sheep, or goats, so it *may* have been possible to avoid eating meat and not be disobeying that commandment. John the Baptist, after all, didn't appear to eat meat much (except for locusts), nor did he displease God. Admittedly, however, the Passover lamb was to be eaten by the whole community of Israel, so at least for that, meat eating was required, to participate in a very important event. (*Ex. 12:46 -47*)

The firstborn clean animal was brought to Jerusalem within a certain two -year period. During the time between birth and the trip to Jerusalem, he had special, set -apart treatment - the firstborn ox was <u>not</u> made to work, and the firstborn sheep was <u>not</u> to be sheared. (Remember, the firstborn animal was God's, not the person's, so the person could not use or profit from the animal.)

(Note: The Passover lamb received similar special treatment, but only for a few days - the lamb was selected on the tenth day of the month, well taken care of, and slaughtered at twilight on the fourteenth day of the month.)

After the special treatment, the firstborn clean animal was brought to Jerusalem, and the whole human family partook in the Firstborn offering feast in the presence of the LORD their God. (*Deut. 15:19-20*)

However, if the firstborn clean animal was defective, it was <u>not</u> to be sacrificed, but it was still to be eaten:

> *Deut. 15:21-22 If a (firstborn) animal has a defect, is lame or blind, or has any serious flaw, you must <u>not</u> sacrifice it to the LORD your God. You are to eat it in your own towns.*

Every two out of three years, the Jews were to <u>eat</u> the tithe (a tenth of their produce) and the firstborn of their herds and flocks before God, in Jerusalem. If they had been bountifully blessed and it was a difficult distance to carry the large tithe, then they were to exchange it for money, go to Jerusalem, and spend it on "*whatever you like: cattle, sheep, wine or other fermented drink, or anything you wish. Then you and your household shall eat there in the presence of the LORD your God and rejoice. And do not neglect the Levites living in your towns, for they have no allotment or inheritance of their own.*" (*Deut. 14:22 -26*) Every third year, the "*year of the tithe*", all their tithes of that year's produce were to be stored in their towns so that the Levites, aliens, orphans, and widows could eat them instead. (*Deut. 14:28-29, Deut. 26:12*)

Future Sacrificial System

There are prophecies written during the Jewish captivity in Babylonia where God says He will bring the Jews back to their land. Some of these prophecies appear to apply not only to the returns that already happened (after Babylonian captivity and after World War II) but also to a future time, because they refer to things not yet come, such as God's glory arriving in Zion after all the nations have suffered the wrath of God; all the nations fearing and serving God and bringing wealth to Zion; a son of David permanently ruling from Jerusalem's throne; and Jerusalem being a place of safety, peace, and prosperity. Some of these prophecies involve the offering of sacrifices, which implies that at least certain kinds will be restored. The apparent support of future biblical sacrifices was hard for me to write here because my love for animals has made me become vegetarian (except for clean fish), but it appears to be true.

It would seem to me that as long as meat continues to be eaten in this world, then in a future sacrificial system it will be proper and still applicable to offer some of it back to God with thanksgiving and rejoicing, as was done with tithes: *"Then you and your household shall eat there in the presence of the LORD your God and rejoice."* (*Deut. 14:26*)

Actually, anytime you eat meat, it should be with rejoicing and thanks to God. Everyone who eats meat has a share in the slaughter and responsibility for the killing and should not be careless about it or take it for granted. It is only right to be very thankful and grateful for the food and products you are getting from the deaths of the animals and God Who provided them to you.

It appears that non -Jews also did and will do offerings in a time to come, much like Noah, Abraham, and Abel did offerings prior to there being Jewish people:

> *(Isa. 56:6-7) And foreigners who bind themselves to the LORD to serve Him, to love the Name of the LORD, and to worship Him, all who keep the Sabbath without desecrating it and who hold fast to My covenant- these I will bring to My holy mountain and give them joy in My house of prayer. Their <u>burnt offerings</u> and <u>sacrifices</u> will be accepted on My altar; for My house will be called a house of prayer for **all the nations**.*

Interestingly, both Noah and Abel were sacrificing animals prior to their officially having been given by God as food after the Flood. One doesn't really know from the Bible if some people were eating meat prior to the Flood, but theoretically after the Fall, with death having entered the world, at least animals had probably started eating other animals.

It would seem that the future sacrifices would be primarily offered in thanks, giving back to and honoring God, and less for redemption, since God accomplished that through His Son's sacrifice (although future sacrifices of blood are mentioned).

There are several references to future offerings and sacrifices. Jeremiah writes of a future restored kingdom before which all nations on earth will be in awe and tremble. I think it applies to the future return from Babylonia at the time Jeremiah wrote it but also a time yet to come, especially since it refers to abundant peace for Jerusalem, restoration of the land itself that has been desolate, and the coming of the Messiah as king. Also, other passages definitely speaking of a time not yet come say very similar things.

Jeremiah - offerings included in the future time:

Jer. 33:9-12, Jer. 33:14-18 " Then this city will bring Me renown, joy, praise and honor before all the nations on earth that hear of all the good things I do for it; and they will be in awe and tremble at the abundant prosperity and peace I provide for it." This is what the LORD says: "You say about this place, 'It is a desolate waste...' Yet in the towns of Judah and the streets of Jerusalem... there will be heard once more the sounds of joy and gladness, the voices of bride and bridegroom, and the voices of those who bring thank offerings *to the house of the LORD, saying, 'Give thanks to the LORD Almighty, for the LORD is good; His love endures forever.'*

For I will restore the fortunes of the land as they were before, says the LORD... In this place, desolate... there will again be pastures for shepherds to rest their flocks... The days are coming... when I will fulfill the gracious promise I made to the house of Israel and to the house of Judah.

'In those days and at that time I will make a righteous Branch sprout from David's line; He will do what is just and right in the land. In those days Judah will be saved and Jerusalem will live in safety. This is the name by which it will be called: The LORD Our Righteousness.' For this is what the LORD says: 'David will never fail to have a man to sit on the throne of the house of Israel, nor will the priests, who are Levites, ever fail to have a man to stand before Me continually to <u>offer burnt offerings, to burn grain offerings and to present sacrifices</u>.'"

Of course, this passage doesn't prove that sin offerings won't be done, but it at least mentions that thank offerings and sacrifices *will* be done. Thank offerings can also be not of animal - they can be of grain, oil, spices, money, etc., besides meat and fat.

Zechariah's prophecies about the coming day of the Lord also include a reference to sacrifices <u>afterward</u>:

Zech. 14:2-9, Zech. 14:11-12, Zech. 14:14, Zech. 14:16, Zech. 14:20-21 I will gather all the nations to Jerusalem to fight against it... Then the LORD will go out and fight against those nations... On that day His feet will stand on the Mount of Olives, east of Jerusalem, and the Mount of Olives will be split in two from east to west, forming a great valley, with half of the mountain moving north and half moving south... Then the LORD my God will come, and all the holy ones with Him.

On that day there will be no light, no cold or frost. It will be a unique day, without daytime or nighttime... On that day living water will flow out from Jerusalem... The LORD will be king over the whole earth... Jerusalem will be secure. This is the plague with which the LORD will strike all the nations that fought against Jerusalem: Their flesh will rot while they are still standing on their feet, their eyes will rot in their sockets, and their tongues will rot in their mouths... The wealth of all the surrounding nations will be collected... Then the survivors from all the nations that have attacked Jerusalem will go up year after year to worship the King, the LORD Almighty, and to celebrate the Feast of Tabernacles... On that day, HOLY TO THE LORD will be inscribed on the bells of the horses, and the cooking pots in the LORD's house will be like the sacred bowls in front of the altar. Every pot in Jerusalem and in Judah will be holy to the LORD Almighty, and all who come <u>to sacrifice</u> will take some of the pots and cook in them.

Malachi, referring also to the day of wrath, references offerings afterward, as well:

Mal. 3:2-4 But who can endure the day of His coming? Who can stand when He appears? For He will be like a refiner's fire... He will purify the Levites and refine them like gold and silver. Then the LORD will have men who will <u>bring offerings</u> in righteousness, and the <u>offerings</u> ... will be acceptable to the LORD, as in days gone by...

Theoretically the offerings of righteousness will be animal, because in Deuteronomy, offerings of righteousness would be "slaughtered" (*Deut. 33:19,* the Hebrew word means "slaughter" but is sometimes translated as "sacrifices").

Other references to sacrifices in the future:

- Isaiah - After the nations suffer the wrath of God, now fear and serve Him, and God's glory arrives in Zion: *"All Kedar's flocks will be gathered to you (Zion), the rams of Nebaioth will serve you; they will be accepted as <u>offerings on My altar,</u> and I will adorn My glorious temple."* (*Isa. 60:7*)
- Ezekiel - Possibly the same future time: *"My servant David will be king over them, and they will all have one shepherd. They will follow My laws and be careful to keep My decrees. They will live in the land I gave to My servant Jacob, the land where your fathers lived. They and their children and their children's children will live there forever, and David my servant will be their prince forever... I will put My sanctuary among them forever. My dwelling place will be with them; I will be their God, and they will be My people. Then the nations will know that I the LORD make Israel holy, when My sanctuary is among them forever... The prince himself is the only one who may sit inside the (sanctuary) gateway to eat in the presence of the LORD... The Levites... may <u>slaughter the burnt offerings and sacrifices</u> for the people... The priests,*

who are Levites and descendants of Zadok...are to stand before Me to offer <u>sacrifices of fat and blood</u>, declares the Sovereign LORD. "They alone are to enter My Sanctuary (inner court)..." The man brought me back to the entrance of the temple, and I saw water coming out from under the threshold of the temple... (It became) a river that I could not cross and was deep enough to swim in... He said to me,..."where the river flows everything will live Fruit trees of all kinds will grow on both banks of the river... Every month they will bear, because the water from the sanctuary flows to them. Their fruit will serve for food and their leaves for healing." This is what the Sovereign LORD says: "...You are to distribute this land among yourselves according to the tribes of Israel. You are to allot it as an inheritance for yourselves and for the aliens who have settled among you and who have children. You are to consider them as native-born Israelites; along with you they are to be allotted an inheritance among the tribes of Israel... And the name of the city from that time on will be: THE LORD IS THERE." (Ezek. 37:24 -28; Ezek. 44:3, Ezek. 44:10 -11, Ezek. 44:15 -16; Ezek. 47:1, Ezek. 47:5, Ezek. 47:9, Ezek. 47:12 -13, Ezek. 47:21 -22; Ezek. 48:35; see also Ezek. 34:23 -24)

Regarding animals, I will only conclude here that in future times, there will be sacrifices again. This book is not meant as any more of an in -depth study than to show basic themes, patterns, and concepts presented throughout the Bible itself concerning the animals.

CHAPTER 6

Flesh and Spirit

Before I proceed, it is only fair to mention that "soul" and "life" are closely related in the biblical texts, and that various cultures and belief systems have differences (or not) between "spirit" and "soul". The points I am making in this book are that the <u>lives</u> of animals are significant in the Bible. Their life force is from God and important to Him. The animals have spirits, and humans have spirits, as will be shown below.

Life in the Blood

Tied into the biblical concept of life is that the life is also in the blood. This has been discussed previously, but now the focus is more detailed, especially as it pertains to the relationship of flesh and spirit.

<u>All</u> mankind (before there were the Jewish people) was instructed early on not to eat blood, because the life (or soul) is in the blood, and man is not to consume

that. As we saw previously, when God first gave meat as food for mankind, God said to Noah and his sons: *"Everything that lives and moves will be food for you… But you must not eat meat that has its lifeblood still in it." (Gen. 9:4)* Clearly, man must not eat blood. Other passages say that slaughterers are to drain the lifeblood from the animal before its flesh may be consumed.

Since at the time God said this to Noah and his sons, He was giving all animals as food, it is clear that the consumption of the blood of <u>any</u> kind of creature is biblically forbidden - the <u>life</u> (or soul) is in the blood, and blood can atone for a <u>life</u>.

Man is to respect the <u>life</u> of the creature he eats by not consuming its lifeblood:

> *Lev. 17:10-11 Any Israelite or any alien living among them who eats any blood- I will set My face against that person who eats blood and will cut him off from his people. For the life of a creature is in the blood, and I have given it to you to make atonement for yourselves on the altar; it is the blood that makes atonement for one's life.*

As you know, animals sacrificed for atonement were also to be clean - certain kinds designated by God and representing purity. However, even when cattle, sheep, and goats were <u>not</u> being sacrificed but only slaughtered for food - the Israelites were still to be very careful with the blood (just as the priests would be):

Deut. 12:20-21, Deut. 12:23-25 When the LORD your God has enlarged your territory as He promised you, and you crave meat and say, "I would like some meat," then you may eat as much of it as you want. If the place where the LORD your God chooses to put His Name is too far away from you, you may slaughter animals from the herds and flocks the LORD has given you, as I have commanded you, and in your own towns you may eat as much of them as you want... But... the <u>blood</u> is the <u>life</u>, and you must not eat the <u>life</u> with the <u>meat</u>. You must not eat the blood; pour it out on the ground like water. Do not eat it, so that it may go well with you and your children after you, because you will be doing what is right in the eyes of the LORD.

After the formal sacrificial system was established, the life and blood of animals and the connection with atonement were so important that if someone <u>sacrificed</u> an animal on his own without a priest, that was considered bloodshed and punishable by banishment. Anyone who sacrificed an ox, sheep, or goat without bringing it to the Tabernacle - that man was to be considered guilty of <u>bloodshed</u>; he had *"shed blood"* (practically murder) and was to be cut off from his people. (*Lev. 17:3 -4*)

All Flesh

I'd like to point out that the Hebrew language does have and use a word that signifies "man" only, such as this verse: *"For the eyes of <u>men</u> and all the tribes of Israel are* *on the LORD." (Zech. 9:1)* The Hebrew here is "adam", which specifically means "man" or "mankind". Yet, the broader words in Hebrew for "all flesh" or "all living creatures", "kol basar", are deliberately used extensively in the Bible.

God is the God of <u>all flesh</u>:

> *Jer. 32:27 (Bible in Basic English) See, I am the Lord, the God of <u>all flesh</u> (some translations: living creatures): is there anything so hard that I am unable to do it?*

Repeatedly, the Bible shows all flesh participating together in seeing the might of God, in punishments, in receiving God's Spirit of life, and in praising Him. This is discussed in other sections of this book, but here are a few additional examples showing scriptures citing "all flesh":

"Be silent, <u>all flesh</u>, before the LORD! For He is roused from His holy habitation." (Zech. 2:17 (JPS Tanakh)) This verse is similar to one in Habakkuk which says for *all the earth* to be silent: *"But the LORD is in His holy temple; let all the earth be silent before Him." (Hab. 2:20)* Other scriptures also mention creation trembling before the awesomeness and power of God.

God visits retribution on all flesh together. We have seen over and over how the animals are included in the misfortunes of the people:

> *Jer. 45:5 (JPS Tanakh) For I am going to bring disaster upon <u>all flesh</u> - declares the LORD.*

All flesh sees and experiences God's great acts together:

Isa. 40:4-5 (KJV) Every valley shall be exalted, and every mountain and hill shall be made low: and the crooked shall be made straight, and the rough places plain: And the glory of the LORD shall be revealed, and all flesh shall see it together: for the mouth of the LORD hath spoken it.

Some translations say "mankind", but it seems pretty apparent that these mighty acts of God will be seen by the animals along with the humans.

It is clear throughout the Bible that God is the God of all His creation, and thus the God of all flesh, mankind and animal, all in whom He has placed His breath of life. He is my God, and the God of my dog, and the God of the wild deer in the woods. We are all His, and He is <u>our</u> God. He creates and gives life to us all:

Eph. 4:4-6 There is... one Lord,...one God and Father of <u>all</u>, Who is over <u>all</u> and through <u>all</u> and in <u>all</u>.

Spirit

Regarding spirit, there are many references in the Bible to the spirits of animals. Animals have the breath of life, and it's frequently mentioned in the same context as humans having the breath of life. And that breath of life is sometimes referred to as the breath of God, which bestows life and *is* life.

The animals were formed out of the ground by God (*Gen. 2:19)*, and they have the breath of life - in Genesis 1:30, the Hebrew words for the breath of life that animals have are "nefesh chayah", most closely translated as "living soul":

> *Gen. 1:29-30 Then God said,... "And to all the beasts of the earth and all the birds of the air and all the creatures that move on the ground - everything that has the <u>breath of life</u>* (some translations: *a <u>living soul</u>) in it, I give every green plant for food."* (Note that this is God being quoted- they're *His* words.)

In Genesis 2:7, the Hebrew words for the breath of life that God breathed into Adam are "nishmat chayim", closely translated as "breath of life":

> *Gen. 2:7 The LORD God formed the man from the dust of the ground and breathed into his nostrils the <u>breath of life</u>, and the man became a living being.*

In both creation cases there is a living soul, and the NIV translators chose to use the words "breath of life" for both animal and man.

And again, during the flood, animals were referred to as having the breath of life. God said He would "*destroy <u>all life</u> under the heavens, every creature that has the <u>breath of life</u> in it.*" (*Gen. 6:17)* And sure enough, the Bible says that "*everything on dry land that had the <u>breath of life</u>* (some translations: *"<u>breath of the **spirit** of life</u>) in its nostrils died... men <u>and animals and the creatures that move along the ground and the birds in the air</u>...*" (*Gen.*

7:22 -23) The Hebrew words for the breath of life here are "nishmat ruach chayim", translated as "breath of the spirit of life". The animals are specifically listed, in the same context as man, altogether, with the exact same words for all. There can be no confusion as to whether only man was being referred to in this way.

In Job, there is an interesting statement that if God were to take His breath back from creation, all men and animals would die together:

Job 34:14-15 (JPS Tanakh) If He but intends it, He can call back His spirit and breath (other translations: soul); all flesh would at once expire, and mankind return to the dust.

This same concept is also stated in the Psalms very beautifully:

Psalm 104:24-25, Psalm 104:27-31 How many are your works, LORD! In wisdom You made them all; the earth is full of Your creatures... Living things both large and small... These all look to You to give them their food at the proper time. When You give it to them, they gather it up; when You open Your hand, they are satisfied with good things. When You hide Your face, they are terrified; **when You take away their breath** (some translations: **"spirit"**), **they die and return to the dust. When You send Your Spirit** (some translations: **"breath"**), **they are created, and You renew the face of the earth.** *May the glory* *of the LORD endure forever; may the LORD rejoice in His works.*

There are those who may find it disturbing to consider animals as having God's breath/spirit of life like humans do, as they fear that this places animals in an equal position to mankind. It does not. There are other things that still place mankind in preeminence to the animals.

One is that man was created in God's image. The importance of that is partly shown in the rule God gave to mankind and the animals, as previously noted: *"And for your lifeblood I will surely demand an accounting. I will demand an accounting from every animal. And from each man, too, I will demand an accounting for the life of his fellow man. 'Whoever sheds the blood of man, by man shall his blood be shed; **for in the image of God has God made man.**'"* (Gen. 9:5 -6)

No animal was given that distinction. It is interesting to note that no man is to murder another man for the same reason - no one, man or animal, should freely kill someone made in the image of God, even when he himself is made in the image of God. The image of God must be honored. Some have said that this even makes suicide wrong to do - human beings - you - are made in the image of God and oh, so precious - so very, very significant and important to God. Be careful in how you treat such beings, even yourself.

In a similar way, other things that place mankind in preeminence to the animals are that man was given rulership over the animals by God, and that he was given a place of honor: *"You made him a little lower than the heavenly beings and crowned him with glory and honor. You made him ruler over the works of your hands; you put everything under his feet: all flocks and herds, and the beasts of the field, the birds of the air, and the fish of the sea, all that swim the paths of the seas." (Psalm 8:5 -9)*

Mankind's rulership (of creation) could be another case to support the rule for animals not to kill humans and humans not to kill humans. We were made <u>rulers</u> by God, and rulers ordained by God are typically not to be killed by just anyone, as David made clear several times when he could've slain King Saul and did not: *"The LORD forbid that I should… lift my hand against him; for he is the anointed of the LORD." (1 Sam. 24:6)* Granted, David was referring to kings selected by God to be anointed, but in a way, God also selected mankind to be rulers too.

So… Mankind, created in God's image, is the ruler of animals, in whom is God's breath of the spirit of life.

Which is more important - the spirit or the fleshly body?

Jesus shows the precedence of spirit over flesh when He says, *"The Spirit gives life, the flesh counts for nothing." (John 6:63)* Indeed, sometimes the breath of life is referred to as the very spirit of <u>God</u>: *"As long as I have life within me, the <u>breath of God</u> (some translations: <u>spirit of God</u>) in my nostrils, my lips will not speak wickedness, and my tongue will utter no deceit." (Job 27:3 -4)* The breath of God is a precious gift of life directly from God's very being, and no one else has ever been able to make something become alive or otherwise explain exactly what causes life. And God's life-giving spirit/breath is in <u>all</u> of His breathing creation - the animals, too.

Sometimes I think about why it is that resting restores oneself. Just being still for a bit can help you build up the energy to do something. Why would inactivity *increase* one's energy? There's no discernable intake of energy, you'd think resting was more like stasis or that energy would continue to deplete. Sometimes I wonder if something like God's life -giving breath is in the very air, that simply breathing God's air in your nostrils restores energy and renews God's living beings. God is all around us. Your body certainly can't live without breath.

There is a proverb that refers to animal "souls" in some translations: *"A righteous man cares for the needs of his animal (some translations: "animal's soul")." (Prov. 12:10)* Some translations leave out the "soul", and in context it does mean the animal, his self, who he is, the needs of his being. But the spirit is the main essence of being. Daniel refers to his spirit as <u>himself</u>, encased in a holder (body), in some translations. *Daniel 7:15* in one translation that closely follows the Hebrew says that Daniel said that his spirit <u>in its sheath</u> was troubled, while another translation says that his spirit <u>deep within him</u> was troubled.

Peter says, *"I live in the tent of this body..."* (*2 Peter 1:13*) And Paul refers to the body as the earthly tent that we (who we are, our core being, our spirits) live in:

> *2 Cor. 4:16, 2 Cor. 4:18- 5:1, 2 Cor. 5:3 Though outwardly we are wasting away, yet inwardly we are being renewed day by day... So we fix our eyes not on what is seen, but on what is unseen. For what is seen is temporary, but what is unseen is eternal. Now we know that if the <u>earthly tent</u> we live in is destroyed, we have a building from God, an eternal house in heaven... For while we are in this tent, (some translations add: our earthly body,) we groan and are burdened, because we do not wish to be unclothed but to be clothed with our heavenly dwelling, so that what is mortal may be swallowed up by life.*

Animals are spirits in bodies too. Some Bible translations say that God is the God of the <u>spirits</u> of <u>all flesh</u>: *"O God, Source of the breath (some translations: <u>spirits</u>) of all <u>flesh</u>!"* (*Num. 16:22* (*JPS Tanakh*)) Some Bibles translate "flesh" here as "humankind". But according to the Hebrew lexicon, the Hebrew words used there *can* mean the flesh of animals and of man. In fact, the first meaning is "all living beings" - "kol <u>basar</u> ": (a) All living beings; (b) Animals; (c) Mankind. Nearby Bible verses use the same words, "kol basar", and specifically clarify "man and animal": *"The first offspring of every womb, both man <u>and animal</u> (same words, kol basar)..."* (*Num. 18:15*, also *Num. 27:16*) Considering that God's breath of life is in all of His breathing creatures, and considering the references discussed here, I am convinced that animals have spirits.

The book of Job mentions the souls (life) of every living thing, even those who do not directly breathe air, such as the fish - God made, and is the giver of life to, all:

> *Job 12:7-10 But ask the animals, and they will teach you; or the birds of the air, and they will tell you; or speak to the earth, and it will teach you, or let the <u>fish of the sea</u> inform you. Which of all these does not know that the hand of the LORD has done this? In His hand is the <u>life</u>* (some translations: <u>*soul*</u>) *<u>of every creature</u> and the breath of all mankind.*

There is a verse in Isaiah that some could point to and say, "But this verse says that horses don't have spirits!" It is this: *"But the Egyptians are men and not God; their horses are flesh and not spirit." (Isa. 31:3)* But the point of this verse is that the mighty ones of Egypt are not God or supernatural spiritual beings - they are only mortal men and their mortal horses (<u>both</u> of whom have spirits, they just aren't powerful spiritual beings). A previous verse clarifies not to trust in Egypt's men and horses rather than God: *"Woe to those who go down to Egypt for help, who rely on horses, who trust... in the great strength of their horsemen, but do not look to the Holy One of Israel, or seek help from the LORD." (Isa. 31:1)*

A body can even have more than one spirit. There is the personal spirit that is the original occupant and owner of the body itself, but other spirits can inhabit it also, such as the Holy Spirit. David pleas: *"Do not... take your Holy Spirit from me". (Psalm 51:11)* He asks for his own spirit to be renewed, and for God to not take away <u>His</u> Holy Spirit.

There are also evil spirits (demons) which can inhabit a living body. As we have seen before, the body is a tent, a sheath, a receptacle for a spirit - good or evil. Bodies that are able to also house evil spirits can be animal as well as human:

> *Matt. 8:28-33 When (Jesus) arrived at the other side in the region of the Gadarenes, two demon-possessed men coming from the tombs met Him. They were so violent that no one could pass that way. "What do You want with us, Son of God?" they shouted. "Have You come here to torture us before the appointed time?"*
>
> *Now some distance from them a large herd of pigs was feeding. The demons begged Jesus, "If You drive us out, send us into the herd of pigs." He said to them, "Go!" So they came out and went into the pigs, and the <u>whole herd</u> rushed down the steep bank into the lake and died in the water.*

Did the pigs not tolerate demons, causing the pigs to drown themselves deliberately to escape? Was it the abruptness or shock of the demons entering the pigs' bodies? One might guess that the demons made the pigs run and drown, but it appears that typically a demon wants a <u>live</u> body to live and rest in: *"When an evil spirit comes out of a man, it goes through arid places <u>seeking rest</u>*

and does not find it. Then it says, 'I will return to the house I left'… Then it goes and takes with it seven other spirits more wicked than itself, and they go in and <u>live there</u>. And the final condition of that man is worse than the first." (*Matt. 12:43 -45*)

On the other hand, there is the reference in Mark where the evil spirit in a boy often tried to kill him: " (*The evil spirit) has often thrown (the boy) into the fire or water to kill him." (Mark 9:22)* That's killing your host, so to speak! So maybe an evil spirit is better off departing a body as it dies (such as going into the pigs or killing its host), rather than being expelled out to no body at all…?

In any case, clearly the pigs' bodies could host the demons, the same as humans, at least initially. It is unclear whether the pigs panicked and drowned themselves or the demons drove them to it.

The book of Ecclesiastes discusses how man and animal are tied together in the fate of death:

Eccl. 3:18-22 I also thought, "As for men, God tests them so that they may see that they are like the animals. Man's fate is like that of the animals; the same fate awaits them both: As one dies, so dies the other. All have the <u>same breath</u> (some translations: *"spirit"); man has no advantage over the animal… All go to the same place; all come from dust, and to dust all return. Who knows if the spirit of man rises upward and if the <u>spirit</u> of the <u>animal</u> goes down into the earth?…*

For who can bring him (man) *to see what will happen after him?"*

It says that man and animal have the same breath (spirit) - surely God's breath of the spirit of life that we have been reviewing. (Note: Hippocrates even thought that all creatures share the same soul, and just the bodies are different.) Regarding the *"man has no advantage over the animal"* passage, the context appears to be regarding being fated to die - man and animal are equally stuck with death at this time, and any attempt to never die is futile.

In the Ecclesiastes passage, the animal's spirit is a given - the question being asked is where does that spirit go at death, not whether there is a spirit at all. After pointing out with much elaboration the sameness of God's creatures' experience (man and animal), the author questions the perception that man's spirit ascends while the animal's spirit descends and concludes that man can't truly see what happens after death. To my mind, this passage does not uphold the perception that only man goes to heaven - it questions and challenges it.

Later on in Ecclesiastes, the author says this:

Eccl. 12:7 The dust returns to the ground it came from, and the spirit returns to God Who gave it.

This is mighty similar to the passage in Job previously referenced, that said that if God called back His spirit and breath, all flesh would expire and return to dust. (*Job 34:14 -15*)

The spirit exists and animates the body, whether it is man or animal. Without it, the body just falls apart.

It seems to me that those in this world who believe only in the physical and don't acknowledge the spiritual are like someone focusing on the science of a musical instrument, like the metal, wires, keys, and sound of a flute, and totally missing the music. How sad!

Regarding animal spirits, it is interesting to contemplate how the Bible depicts multiple incidents of horses of fire coming from heaven. This could itself imply that there are animals in heaven in spiritual form. For example, when Elijah went up to heaven in a whirlwind, he was first separated from Elisha by a chariot of fire and horses of fire that had appeared, while Elijah ascended to heaven in a whirlwind. (*2 Kings 2:11*) At a later time when the city of Dothan was surrounded by an army out to capture Elisha, and his servant was afraid, the Lord opened the servant's eyes to see that the hills were full of horses and chariots of fire all around Elisha. (*2 Kings 6:17*)

There is also mention of the armies of heaven riding horses in Revelation. Now admittedly there is symbolism all through Revelation that may or may not be truly manifested someday, but at the least, horses are used for it. John says, "*I saw heaven standing open and there before me was a white horse, whose rider is called Faithful and True….The armies of heaven were following Him, riding on white horses.." (Rev. 19:11, Rev. 19:14)* We can at least consider that the Bible at times depicts horses in a spiritual form.

Even more of a wonderment is that the prophets and the book of Revelation speak of four living creatures who are **closest** to the presence of God. These creatures not only have the face of a man but also the faces of animals - the face of a lion, the face of an ox, and the face of an eagle. It's interesting to note that the basic form is like a man, though (the image of God?). Ezekiel says that the very throne of the LORD was over the heads of these creatures:

> *Ezek. 1:5-6, Ezek. 1:10, Ezek. 1:26-29 In the fire was what looked like four living creatures. In appearance their form was that of a man, but each of them had four faces and four wings… Their faces looked like this: Each of the four had the face of a man, and on the right side each had the face of a lion, and on the left the face of an ox; each also had the face of an eagle… Above the expanse over their heads was what looked like a throne of sapphire, and high above on the throne was a figure like that of a man. I saw that from what appeared to be His waist up He looked like glowing metal, as if full of fire, and that from there down He looked like fire; and brilliant light surrounded Him. Like the appearance of a rainbow…, so was the radiance around Him. This was the appearance of the likeness of the glory of the LORD. When I saw it, I fell facedown.*

And Revelation 4 says that in the **center**, around the throne of God Himself, were the four living creatures with animal and human faces:

Rev. 4:2-3, Rev. 4:6-11 There before me was a throne in heaven with someone sitting on it. And the One Who sat there had the appearance of jasper and carnelian. A rainbow, resembling an emerald, encircled the throne... In the <u>center</u>, around the throne, were four living creatures... The first living creature was like a lion, the second was like an ox, the third had a face like a man, and the fourth was like a flying eagle... Day and night they never stop saying: "Holy, holy, holy is the Lord God Almighty, Who was, and is, and is to come." Whenever the living creatures give glory, honor and thanks to Him Who sits on the throne and Who lives for ever and ever, the twenty-four elders fall down before Him Who sits on the throne and worship Him Who lives for ever and ever. They lay their crowns before the throne and say: "You are worthy, our Lord and God, to receive glory and honor and power, for You created all things, and by Your will they were created and have their being."

So the beings closest to God on His throne have both animal and human aspects, and God is praised for creating <u>all</u> things and giving them their being. I have not studied lore on the four living beings and shall not discuss them further here, apart from pointing out that such creatures are in the very closest presence of God.

CHAPTER 7

God Saves

This book is not a thorough dissertation on all the intricacies of salvation for mankind or a deep look at what salvation entails. I did however carefully consider references to spiritual salvation for individual humans, and references to God saving the whole creation, and came to the conclusion that God through Jesus saves and will renew all things, including His animals as part of His creation, while also noting that there is much more depth and information regarding what God expects on a personal level from mankind. Humans must turn from evil and to God, choosing and accepting (and yes, loving) Him, while the animals already know God and look to God for their help and sustenance, trusting the One Who holds their lives in His hands. I will try to explain further what led me to this conclusion. Although some references to salvation can be read two ways (as "saved from troubles in the world" or as "saved forever"), you will see a pattern and some references that as a whole point to both - that God is the Savior of all, now and forever, and <u>all</u> Who trust in Him shall praise Him for it!

All Look to God to be Saved

God is the God of our salvation, saving those who trust in Him. The Psalms praise God for His loving kindness and say that God saves both man and beast. Jewish liturgy recites that God saves both man and beast. Psalm 36 says:

> *Psalm 36:5-7, Psalm 36:9 Your love, O LORD, reaches to the heavens, Your faithfulness to the skies. Your righteousness is like the mighty mountains, Your justice like the great deep. O LORD, You <u>preserve</u>* (some translations: *"<u>save</u>") <u>both man and beast</u>. How priceless is Your unfailing love!...For with You is the <u>fountain of life</u>.*

If God's kindness is so bountiful and full that it reaches to the heavens, it seems that He would not limit Himself to only saving humans. He didn't limit Himself for the Flood, He saved all kinds of animals then too, which took a lot more effort than just saving man. God carefully planned and crafted each kind of creature, tiny and huge, and put His breath of life into each one. They're all His - and who willingly parts with things he has personally created and cared for, and put himself into?

David's Psalm 145 also beautifully states how God loves and cares for all of His creation and <u>saves</u> those who cry out to Him and rely on Him. The animals take refuge in God and look to Him to sustain and save them:

*Psalm 145:9-10, Psalm 145:13, Psalm 145:15-16, Psalm 145:18-19, Psalm 145:21 The LORD is good to all; He has compassion on <u>all</u> He has made. <u>All</u> You have made will praise You, O LORD…The LORD is…loving toward <u>all</u> He has made… The eyes of <u>all</u> look to You, and You give them their food at the proper time. You open Your hand and satisfy the desires of <u>every living thing</u>… The LORD is near to <u>all</u> who call on Him… He fulfills the desires of those who fear Him; He hears their cry and **<u>saves</u>** them… Let every <u>creature</u> praise His holy Name <u>forever and ever</u>.*

God saves those who call on Him, and David speaks of <u>every creature</u> praising God **forever and ever.**

Job talks about how God deeply cares for His creatures and does not want to part with them. He also says to God: *"I will wait for my renewal to come. You will call and I will answer You; You will long for the creature Your hands have made." (Job 14:14 -15)* Clearly Job is referring to himself, here, but God loves all His creatures that He so carefully and exquisitely made, so I think He would long for and renew all of them at the renewal of "all things".

Peter says that God is not wanting anyone to perish (but that all humans come to repentance). (*2 Peter*

3:9) I propose that God does not want His animals, Whom He knows intimately and who know Him, to perish either.

In some Bible translations, *Hebrews 2:10* calls God the Creator and <u>Preserver</u> of <u>everything</u>.

We have seen how God is the God of the animals too and knows them and cares for them. And they rely on God, trust in God, and come to Him. David says to God:

> *Psalm 65:2, Psalm 65:5 O You Who hear prayer, to You all men (* some translations: <u>*all living creatures*</u>*) come... You answer us with awesome deeds of righteousness, O God our S <u>avior</u>, the hope of <u>all</u> the ends of the earth (* some translations: *in Whom <u>all</u> put their trust, to the ends of the earth) and of the farthest seas...*

And David exhorts: *"Your love, O LORD, <u>endures forever</u> - do not abandon the works* (some translations: <u>*creatures*</u>*) of Your hands." (Psalm 138:8)*

> *Psalm 34:22* says of the Lord that *"no one will be condemned who takes refuge in Him."*

God says: *"Turn to Me and be saved, all you ends of the earth; for I am God, and there is no other. By Myself I have sworn..: Before Me <u>every</u> knee will bow; by Me <u>every</u> tongue will swear. They will say of Me, 'In the LORD alone are righteousness and strength.'" (Isa. 45:22 -24)*

Psalm 22:29 says that all who go down to the dust will kneel before Him. And Paul says of Jesus, *"Therefore God exalted Him to the highest place and gave Him the name that is above every name, that at the name of Jesus every knee should bow, in heaven and on earth and under the earth, and every tongue confess that Jesus Christ is Lord, to the glory of God the Father." (Phil. 2:9-11)*

Alone, the above quotes would appear to indicate that only humans will do this, and indeed, the main point of them is that every human, who denied God and Jesus or had faith in them, will acknowledge them. However, every animal will acknowledge them both as well, as is clearly stated in Revelation: *"Then I heard <u>every creature</u> in heaven and on earth and under the earth and on the sea, and <u>all</u> that is in them, singing: 'To Him who sits on the throne and to the Lamb be praise and honor and glory and power, for ever and ever!' The four living creatures said 'Amen.'" (Rev. 5:13 -14)*

The story of Jonah and Nineveh illustrates how God has compassion and salvation for the animals as well as for the humans. Knowing how all of God's living creatures together were dependent on God and the hope of His mercy, and that both the animals and the humans would suffer God's wrath together, the king of Nineveh specified that both man <u>and animal</u> should deny themselves and call out to God:

Jonah 3:7-8, Jonah 3:10 (JPS Tanakh) "No man <u>or beast</u>- of <u>flock or herd</u>- shall taste anything! They shall *not graze, and they shall not drink water! They shall be covered with sackcloth- man <u>and beast</u>- and shall cry mightily to God."* (The animals, too!)...*God saw what they did, how they were turning back from their evil ways. And God renounced the punishment He had planned to bring upon them, and did not carry it out.*

When responding to Jonah's anger about God relenting, God Himself specifically mentioned the very young humans <u>and the animals</u> as reasons to have pity and not cause harm:

Jonah 4:11 (JPS Tanakh) And should I not care about Nineveh, that great city, in which there are more than a hundred and twenty thousand persons who do not know their right hand from their left, and <u>many beasts as well</u>!

Both the persons <u>and the beasts</u> were reasons for God to have pity. I think the "persons" reference is to toddlers and infants because of their lack of basic knowledge (right hand vs. left hand) and because of the size of the city: *"Now Nineveh was a very great town, three days' journey from end to end." (Jonah 3:3, Bible in Basic English).* Nave's Topical Bible says that a day's journey in those days was 18 -20 miles. So I figure that the city could've been as large as 60 miles across. Even if there were pastures and fields within the city, the city's great size allowed for a huge number of people, with 120,000 being the very young. So God was especially considering the beasts and the very young children.

The story of Nineveh illustrates people <u>and animals</u> calling out to God and then being saved. There are many biblical texts referring to calling out to God or trusting in Him and being saved:

> *Psalm 98:3-4, Psalm 98:7-9 <u>All the ends of the earth</u> have seen the <u>salvation</u> of our God. Shout for joy to the LORD, <u>all the earth</u>, burst into jubilant song with music… Let the sea resound, and everything in it, the world, and <u>all</u> who live in it. Let the rivers clap their hands, let the mountains sing together for joy; let them sing before the LORD, for He comes to judge the earth.*

> *Acts 2:20-21 The sun will be turned to darkness and the moon to blood before the coming of the great and glorious day of the Lord. And everyone who calls on the name of the Lord will be saved.*

> *Rom. 10:12-13 The same Lord is Lord of all and richly blesses all who call on Him, for, "Everyone who calls on the Name of the Lord will be saved."*

God is a God who saves. He is all about saving the world and glorifying Himself (and power to Him, I say!). King Darius wrote: *"People must fear and reverence the God of Daniel. For He is the living God and He endures forever; His kingdom will not be destroyed, His dominion will never end. He <u>rescues and He saves</u>…" (Daniel 6:26 -27)* David says: *"Praise be to the Lord, to God our Savior, Who daily bears our burdens. Our God is a God who <u>saves</u>; from the Sovereign LORD comes <u>escape from death</u>." (Psalm 68:19 -20)*

Psalm 68 does go on to say that surely God will crush His enemies, though - humans who deliberately shut God out and choose to stay in their sin, will perish: *"Surely God will crush the heads of His <u>enemies</u>, the hairy crowns of those who go on* (some translations: *"continue"*, *"saunter"*) *in their sins." (Psalm 68:21)*

> *Deut. 32:35-36, Deut. 32:39-41, Deut. 32:43 (The LORD said) "It is Mine to avenge; I will repay."... The LORD will judge His people and have compassion on His servants... "See now that I Myself am He! There is no god besides me. I put to death and I bring to life, I have wounded and I will heal, and no one can deliver out of my hand... As surely as I live forever, when I sharpen My flashing sword and My hand grasps it in judgment, I will take vengeance on My <u>adversaries</u> and repay <u>those who hate Me</u>."... Rejoice, oh nations, with His people, for He will avenge the blood of His servants; He will take <u>vengeance on His enemies</u> and <u>make atonement</u> for His <u>land</u> and people.*

God will make atonement for His <u>land</u> and people. References to land generally include the animals who inhabit it along with the humans.

He will ultimately take vengeance on His enemies, those who hate Him, while saving those who call on Him. Nowhere in the Bible did I see animals hating God or opposing Him. I would think they are not His enemies. It is the humans who reject God and love wickedness who are His adversaries:

2 Thes. 2:10 They perish because they <u>refused</u> to love the truth and so be saved.

2 Thes. 2:12 All will be condemned who have not believed the truth but have <u>delighted in wickedness</u>.

Psalm 145:20 The LORD watches over <u>all</u> who love Him, but all the wicked He will destroy.

It appears that God through Jesus saves <u>the world</u>, but humans can choose to reject God and His salvation, and deliberately stay in their sin. Humans are called upon to turn from their sin and accept God and His salvation. Mankind, through Adam, caused the Fall which all living creatures bear the consequences of, and although the world is redeemed through the sacrifice of one man, Jesus the Messiah, mankind is still responsible to <u>choose</u> God and salvation, just as mankind originally <u>chose</u> disobedience and consequently, death. The animals are carried along in the Fall <u>and</u> in the redemption, but humans of sound mind must individually turn from man's original choice and turn to God and His salvation in order to have eternal life.

Man has free choice and personal responsibility - he can reject God, Jesus, and salvation.

John 3:36 Whoever believes in the Son has eternal life, but whoever <u>rejects</u> the Son will not see life, for God's wrath remains on him.

2 Cor. 5:19-20…God was reconciling the <u>world</u> to Himself in Christ, not counting men's sins against them… We are … ambassadors, as though God were *making His appeal through us. We implore you on Christ's behalf: Be reconciled to God.*

*John 12:47-50 (Bible in Basic English) (Jesus said:) "I did not come to be judge of the world but to give <u>salvation to the **world**</u>. He who <u>puts me on one side and does not take my words to heart,</u> is not without a judge: the word which I have said will be his judge on the last day. For I have not said it on my authority, but the Father who sent Me gave me orders what to say and how to say it. And I have knowledge that His order (some translations: "command") is <u>eternal life</u>."*

God the Father's command is eternal life! Humans can reject God and Jesus and what They offer, but otherwise, God, through Jesus, saves the world. Jesus' very name means "God <u>saves</u>".

John 3:14-17 (Bible in Basic English) (Jesus answered:) "As the snake was lifted up by Moses in the waste land, even so it is necessary for the Son of man to be lifted up: So that whoever has faith may have in Him eternal life. For God had such love for the <u>world</u> that He gave His only Son, so that whoever has faith in Him may not come to destruction but have eternal life. God did not send his Son into the world to be judge of the world; He sent Him so that the <u>world</u> might have <u>salvation</u> through Him."

John 3:18 (NIV) Whoever believes in Him is not condemned. (Some translations: " Those who trust in him are not judged.")

Sometimes the word "trust" is used in place of the most common translation of "believe" - "trust" is one of the definitions in Bauer's Greek -English lexicon which also mentions that it can mean "to have confidence in", and "to give credence to", much like the meaning of "believe". We have previously seen that the Bible states that the animals look to God for food and help, so I would like to submit that they ultimately <u>trust</u> in God, and they do not turn away from, ignore, or reject Him.

Paul wrote: "*For as in Adam **all** die, so in Christ **all** will be made alive… The last enemy to be <u>destroyed</u> is death.*" *(1 Cor. 15:22, 1 Cor. 15:26)* Death will be eliminated! This isn't conditional, only the death that humans had to suffer, but death <u>itself</u> - the death that was brought into the world at the Fall, that all creation, including the animals, became subject to. <u>All</u> who suffered death will be released from it. But for <u>mankind</u>, after judgment, although some will have life, in its abundant, good sense, those who reject God will have something else: "*Multitudes who sleep in the dust of the earth will awake: some to everlasting life, others to shame and everlasting contempt.*" *(Daniel 12:2)*

> *Prov. 24:19-21 Do not fret because of evil men or be envious of the wicked, for the evil man has no future hope, and the lamp of the wicked will be snuffed out. Fear the LORD…*

To the Romans, Paul wrote:

Rom. 8:19-23 (Bible in Basic English) For the strong desire of <u>every living thing</u> is waiting for the revelation of the sons of God. For <u>every living thing</u> was put under the power of change, not by its desire, but by him who made it so, in <u>hope</u> that <u>all living things</u> will be <u>made free from the power of death</u> and <u>will have a part</u> with the free children of God <u>in glory</u>. For we are conscious that <u>all living things</u> are weeping and sorrowing in pain together till now. And not only so, but we who have the first fruits of the Spirit, even we have sorrow in our minds, waiting for… the <u>salvation of our bodies</u>.

Every living thing, including the animals, was given hope that it will be set free from death and enjoy the freedom and salvation that God's children will have! This shows that God's children (humans who accept and love Him) and creation (including the animals), will all be set free from death.

It is also important to note that creation was not made subject to suffering and pain willingly - <u>it</u> did not make the choice to counter God. <u>Man</u> made the choice to counter God, and creation suffers the consequences because of man who subjected it. In the same manner, creation will be set free from death by the man who saves the world, Jesus the Messiah.

The Bible specifically mentions that many animals will dwell in the restored, new Jerusalem on earth, when God comes to live in the city: "*Jerusalem will be a city* *without walls because of the great number of men **and livestock** (some translations: "**animals**") in it. And I Myself will be a wall of fire around it," declares the LORD, "and I will be its glory within." (Zech. 2:4 -5)* God will be the glory within His city that is filled with people <u>and animals</u>.

Everything in heaven and earth, all things (including the animals) will be under Jesus' headship. Paul wrote:

Eph. 1:9-10, Eph. 1:22-23 He made known to us the mystery of His will according to <u>His good pleasure</u>... to be put into effect when the times will have reached their fulfillment- to bring <u>all things</u> in heaven and on earth together under one head, even Christ... And God placed <u>all things</u> under His feet and appointed Him to be head over everything for the church, which is His body, the fullness of Him Who <u>fills everything</u> (some translations: *"<u>all creation</u>") in every way.*

God fills all creation, and as mentioned previously, all living beings, including the animals, were created <u>for Him</u> (not just for man's use, as some would say):

Col. 1:16-17 For by Him all things were created... All things were created by Him and <u>for Him</u>. He is before all things, and in Him all things hold together.

We and the animals all were created for God, and He's not about to let us go - He and Jesus have gone to great trouble to save and sustain us all! In <u>wisdom</u> God made us <u>all</u>, and not only does creation praise God, but <u>God</u> rejoices in His creation:

Psalm 104:24, Psalm 104:31 How many are your works, O LORD! In wisdom You made them <u>all</u>; the earth is full of your <u>creatures</u> ...May the glory of the LORD endure forever; <u>may the LORD rejoice in His works</u>. Why would God eliminate anything that He rejoices in? Would He not save and keep it?

Col. 1:19-20 For God was pleased to have all His fullness dwell in (His Son) and through Him to <u>reconcile</u> to Himself <u>all things</u>, whether things on earth or things in heaven, by making peace through His blood, shed on the cross.

That would be, <u>all things</u>.

1 Chron. 16:23 Sing to the LORD, <u>all the earth</u>; proclaim His <u>salvation</u> day after day.

Seek God

Creation was given a reliable hope that it too would be set free from death and enjoy the freedom of God's children. And the animals know and call on God. But since man is responsible to turn to God and accept his salvation, humans must begin by seeking God.

David said that the wicked man says "There is no God" and that the wicked man does not seek Him:

Psalm 14:1 The fool says in his heart, "There is no God."

Psalm 10:4, Psalm 10:11, Psalm 10:13 In his pride the wicked does not <u>seek</u> Him; in all his thoughts there *is no room for God... He says to himself, "God has forgotten; He covers His face and never sees..." Why does the wicked man revile God? Why does he say to himself, "He won't call me to account"?*

The animals, however, already have a relationship with God, crying out to Him and trusting in Him. They don't have to go looking for Him, they already <u>know</u> Him and depend on Him:

Job 12:7-10 But ask the animals, and they will teach you; or the birds of the air, and they will tell you; or speak to the earth, and it will teach you, or let the fish of the sea inform you. Which of all these does not <u>know</u> that the hand of the LORD has done this?

Psalm 104:21, Psalm 104:24-25, Psalm 104:27-29 The lions roar for their prey and seek their food from God... The earth is full of Your creatures... living things both large and small... These all look to You to give them their food at the proper time. When You give it to them, they gather it up; when You open Your hand, they are satisfied with good things. When You hide Your face, they are terrified...

Paul emphasizes how near God is to all humans in a similar way, if only they would look for Him: "*God did this so that men would <u>seek Him</u> and perhaps <u>reach out for Him and find Him</u>, though He is <u>not far</u> from each one of us.* **For in Him we live and move and have our being**.*" (Acts 17:27 -28)* So God wants humans, already held alive by Him just like the animals are, to seek and reach out to Him (to want Him, really, to love Him, and to turn away from ways that reject Him), while the animals already know God and look to Him with hope.

So... God wants humans to seek Him and desire Him. Moses said,

"If ... you seek the LORD your God, you will find Him if you look for Him with <u>all</u> your heart and with <u>all</u> your soul." (Deut. 4:29) This is talking about TRULY seeking Him, as in WANTING to find Him. It's not "try experiments or tests to see if God is there, and you will find Him". It is " **s eek** " (as in whole -heartedly LOOK for, with a deep desire to find) and <u>you will find</u>.

Proverbs says: *"If you call out for insight and cry aloud for understanding, and if you <u>look</u> for it <u>as for silver</u> and <u>search</u> for it <u>as for hidden treasure</u>, then you will understand the fear of the LORD and <u>find</u> the knowledge of God."* (Prov. 2:3-5)

When I was a teenager and going to community college, I was bombarded with the message that science alone was real and absolute and there was no God. Having been raised a Christian, I became more and more depressed by the possibility that there might be no God. Finally, one afternoon I went upstairs toward my bedroom, and when I got to the room before mine, I started crying, and facing the wall, I said something like this, <u>from my heart</u>, "God, if you're not there, I guess it doesn't hurt to be talking to a wall. But I don't WANT it to be just the wall, I WANT you to exist! I <u>want</u> there to be the loving God I was taught to know, who cares about us and saves us. I want the stories to be true. I can't stand the thought of you not being there. Oh, please, I want you to be there. Help me <u>know</u> you're there!"

And then the most amazing thing happened - it felt like love was pouring from the walls - I was surrounded by an overflowing huge FLOOD of love from all sides of the room and was filled with the <u>complete</u> <u>assurance</u> that God was there, and he <u>loved</u> me - really, really, <u>really</u> loved me. It was so deeply warm and comforting! I remember taking the final steps into my bedroom, continuing to be engulfed by absolutely overwhelming love, lying down on my bed, and in great relief and release instantly falling asleep. I came out of that experience knowing two things: God *does* exist; and, God is Love. Oh boy, is He Love, with a capital L!

Hebrews 11:6 God... rewards those who <u>earnestly</u> seek Him.

Psalm 70:4 May all who <u>seek</u> You rejoice and be glad in You.

Psalm 105:3-4 Let the hearts of those who <u>seek</u> the LORD rejoice. Look to the LORD and His strength; <u>seek</u> His face always.

Psalm 9:10 Those who know Your Name will trust in You, for You, LORD, have never forsaken those who <u>seek</u> You.

Amos 5:4, Amos 5:6, Amos 5:14 Seek Me and <u>live</u> ...Seek the LORD and <u>live</u> ... Seek good, not evil, *that you may <u>live</u>. Then the LORD Almighty <u>will be</u> <u>with you…</u>*

Love God

God is Love, and His higher creatures have a great capacity for love. There are countless examples of animals loving each other and especially loving humans, even to the highest expression of it, giving their lives for others. Animal parents do it for their young, and some animals such as dogs and cattle have sacrificed their lives to save their humans. *"Greater love has no one than this, that he lay down his life for his friends." (John 15:13)*

The greatest commandments are to love God and to love others. Jesus was asked what one must do to inherit eternal life, and He had the asker give his own assessment from scripture, which was to love the Lord your God with all your heart and with all your soul and with all your strength and with all your mind, and to love your neighbor as yourself. Jesus replied that he had answered correctly - do this and you will <u>live</u>. (*Luke 10:25 -28)*

Animals have the capacity for love and an awareness of and trust in God their creator as has been discussed previously. And God cares about and loves each one of them. *"Are not five sparrows sold for two pennies? Yet not one of them is forgotten by God." (Luke 12:6)*

And there is the example of the peaceable kingdom spoken of by Isaiah, where the earth will be full of the knowledge of God, and the animals, having that knowledge of God and <u>knowing</u> His commandments to love Him and others, will behave in a loving way with one another and with mankind. (*Isa. 11:6 -9*)

> *1 Cor. 2:9 No eye has seen, no ear has heard, no mind has conceived what God has prepared for those who <u>love</u> Him.*

Fear God

The Bible repeatedly speaks of the fear of the Lord and how that is a desired aspect of man's <u>and creation's</u> relationship with God. Fear can be a healthy respect. People both love and fear a great and powerful king who is just and good. Fear at one level can be of pain or something unpleasant, but in the case of fearing God, it is also being in deep awe of and having profound reverence for God and everything that He is. You see God in all His creation, in everything that has the life that He gives it.

In healthy relationships, children both love and fear their father. Their father is so much stronger, more capable, and able to punish wrong. He is their protector, which means enemies have reason to fear him too. He is seen to provide and deny as he chooses. He is powerful, and their lives are in his hands - how much more so with God and <u>all</u> His creation! He is the <u>Father</u> Who made us.

Isa. 64:8 O LORD, You are our Father. We are the clay, You are the potter; we are <u>all</u> the work of Your hand.

Fear of God is first inspired by the knowledge of His vast superiority and might, and the animals experience this too. The Psalmist says:

*Psalm 33:6-8 By the word of the LORD were the heavens made, their starry host by the breath of His mouth. He gathers the waters of the sea into jars; He puts the deep into storehouses. Let <u>all the earth</u> **fear** the LORD.*

When all flesh is silent before the Lord in His holy temple, and when the earth trembles at the coming of the Lord, that is <u>all</u> creatures being in awe and fear of the Lord:

Hab. 2:20 But the LORD is in His holy temple; let <u>all the earth</u> be silent before Him.

Psalm 96:9 Worship the LORD in the splendor of His holiness; tremble before Him, <u>all the earth</u>.

But there is so much more to fearing God than that! The Bible says that God has mercy on and saves those who fear Him, and that includes animals as well as humans:

Psalm 145:15-16, Psalm 145:19, Psalm 145:21 The eyes of <u>all</u> look to You, and You give them their food at the proper time. You open Your hand and satisfy the desires of <u>every living thing</u> … The LORD… fulfills *the desires of those who **fear** Him; He hears their cry and <u>saves</u> them… Let <u>every creature</u> praise His holy name for ever and ever.*

*Psalm 147:9, Psalm 147:11 He provides food for the cattle and for the young ravens when they call… The LORD delights in those who **fear** Him, who put their hope in His unfailing love.*

*Psalm 33:18-19 But the eyes of the LORD are on those who **fear** Him, on those whose hope is in His unfailing love, to <u>deliver them from death</u> and keep them alive in famine…*

*Psalm 85:9 Surely His <u>salvation</u> is near those who **fear** Him.*

*Luke 1:50 His <u>mercy</u> extends to those who **fear** Him.*

Those who fear God are those whom His salvation is near, those upon whom is His mercy. God even uses affliction and trial to get people to turn to Him. Their fearing Him places them in a position to turn to Him and be saved.

Some of the difficult and bad situations you experience are meant to bring you closer to God. People in trouble and hardship turn to God far more readily than people for whom everything is going well, where life is easy, they feel strong, and they're focused on enjoying themselves. There are passages in the Bible where God says that bad things and trials He has put people through were to get their attention, to get them to turn back to Him, to seek Him (not to turn away from Him or ignore Him):

Jer. 32:33 They turned their backs to Me and not their faces; <u>though I taught them again and again</u>, they would not listen or respond to <u>discipline</u>.

Hag. 2:17 "I struck all the work of your hands with blight, mildew and hail, <u>yet you did not turn to Me</u>", declares the LORD.

Isa. 9:13 Yet for all this, His anger is not turned away, His hand is still upraised. <u>But the people have not returned to Him Who struck them</u>, nor have they sought the LORD Almighty.

Amos 4:6-12 "I gave you empty stomachs in every city and lack of bread in every town, <u>yet you have not returned to Me</u>," declares the LORD. "I also withheld rain from you when harvest was still three months away... People staggered from town to town for water but did not get enough to drink, <u>yet you have not returned to Me</u>," declares the LORD. "Many times I struck your gardens and vineyards, I struck them with blight and mildew. Locusts devoured your fig and olive trees, <u>yet you have not returned to Me</u>," declares the LORD. "I sent plagues among you as I did to Egypt. I killed your young men with the sword, along with your captured horses. I filled your nostrils with the stench of your camps, <u>yet you have not returned to Me</u>," declares the LORD. "I overthrew some of you as I overthrew Sodom and Gomorrah. You were like a burning stick snatched from the fire, <u>yet you have not returned to Me</u>," declares the LORD. "Therefore this is what I

*will do to you, Israel, and because I will do this to you,
prepare to meet your God, O Israel."*

Sometimes I wonder if God's Day of Wrath will come
when the majority of people ignore and reject Him, and
do not fear Him. At least in the past, although there
have been different belief systems for how to believe in
and follow God, there was acknowledgement of and
belief in Him. Perhaps when the modern world reaches
a place where most people are turned away from God,
not truly seeking or honoring Him at all, that's when
He will rather drastically get the world's attention!

God is to be feared and also sought for help - He is the
one Who can save, and He has mercy on those who fear
Him and does save them.

*Isa. 8:13-14 The LORD Almighty is the One you are
to regard as holy, He is the One you are to **fear**, He is
the One you are to dread, and He will be a <u>sanctuary</u>.*

When you fear God, when you have absolute respect
for Him and are in total awe of Him, He will be
your sanctuary! Some Psalms even show that fear and
rejoicing are tied together. There is trembling and
jubilation all at once, for all of creation, <u>all</u> that is in it!

*Psalm 96:1-2, Psalm 96:4, Psalm 96:9, Psalm 96:11-
13 Sing to the LORD a new song; sing to the LORD,
<u>all the earth</u>... Proclaim His <u>salvation</u> day after day...
For great is the LORD and most worthy of praise; He
is to be **<u>feared</u>** above all gods.... Worship the LORD
in the splendor of His holiness; **<u>tremble</u>** before Him,*

all the earth ... Let the heavens <u>rejoice</u>, let the earth be <u>glad</u>; let the sea resound, <u>and all that is in it</u>; let the fields be <u>jubilant</u>, <u>and everything in them</u>. Then all the trees of the forest will sing for <u>joy</u>; they will sing before the LORD, for He comes...

There is even delight in fearing God: *"The Spirit of the LORD will rest on him - the Spirit of wisdom and of understanding, the Spirit of counsel and of power, the Spirit of knowledge and of the **fear** of the LORD - and he will **<u>delight in the fear of the LORD</u>**." (Isa. 11:2 -3)*

*Psalm 67:1-2, Psalm 67:4, Psalm 67:6-7 May God be gracious to us and bless us and make His face shine upon us, that Your ways may be known on earth, Your salvation among all the nations... May the nations be glad and sing for **joy**, for You rule the peoples justly and guide the nations of the earth... Then the land will yield its harvest, and God, our God, will bless us. God will bless us, and <u>all the ends of the earth will **fear** Him</u>.*

Sometimes it is seen as a travesty when God allows good people to die. But Isaiah shows that sometimes it is to take them beyond the trials of this world to a place of safety, peace, and rest:

*Isa. 57:1-2 The righteous perish, and no one ponders it in his heart; devout men are taken away, and no one understands that **the righteous are taken away to be spared from evil**. Those who walk uprightly enter into peace; they find rest as they lie in death.*

I think that this could be a reason why the life span of dogs and other pets seems so short to us. Perhaps God has it so that they don't have to spend as much time in this world with its evils as humans do, and so He takes them out of it to a better place after a shorter amount of time than humans endure.

For those who do <u>not</u> fear God, it is a different matter. I think that generally, creation does fear God, but there are *humans* of free will who choose not to fear Him but instead avoid and reject Him, choosing their own wicked way and not choosing good. Solomon wrote: "*...I am certain that it will be well for those who go in **fear** of God and are in **fear** before Him.*" (Eccl. 8:12 (Bible in Basic English)) But he also wrote: "*Yet because the wicked do **not fear** God, it will <u>not</u> go well with them.*" (Eccl. 8:13)

When one does fear and love God, the outcome is to choose right and to do what God wants. Peter said, "*I now realize how true it is that God does not show favoritism but accepts men from every nation who **fear** Him and <u>do what is right</u>.*" (Acts 10:34 -35)

Jesus said: "*Whoever <u>does God's will</u> is My brother and sister and mother.*" (Mark 3:35)

Jesus also said that at the judgment, regarding doing what God wants (caring for others), He will say: "*'Whatever you did not do for one of the least of these, you did not do for Me.' Then they will go away to eternal punishment, but the righteous* (some translations: *"those*

who have <u>done what God wants</u>") will go to eternal life."
(Matt. 25:45-46)

John wrote: *"The world and its desires pass away, but the
man who <u>does the will of God</u> lives forever." (1 John 2:17)*

And what is God's will for humans of free will to choose?
*"He has showed you, O man, what is good. And what does
the LORD require of you? To act justly and to love mercy
and to walk humbly with your God." (Micah 6:8)*

In your life, do you seek, love, and fear the One who
made and sustains you and all creation? Do you love
and treat others as you would have them do to you?

Knowledge of God

*Prov. 2:5 Then you will understand the fear of the
LORD and find the <u>knowledge</u> of God.*

We have seen how the fear of God and the knowledge of
God are tied together. The animals all know God (*Job
12:7-10*, etc.). They already look to God for sustenance
and cry out to God for help and food.

Knowing God ultimately results in doing what God
wants and following His ways. And ultimately, the
animals will have full knowledge of God along with
the people. There are several scriptures about this - note
how the animals will have the full <u>knowledge</u> of the
LORD and of His law of love:

*Isa. 11:6-9 The wolf will live with the lamb, the leopard will lie down with the goat, the calf and the lion and the yearling together; and a little child will lead them. The cow will feed with the bear, their young will lie down together, and the lion will eat straw like the ox. The infant will play near the hole of the cobra, and the young child put his hand into the viper's nest. They will neither harm nor destroy on all My holy mountain, for the <u>earth</u> will be full of the **knowledge** of the LORD as the waters cover the sea.*

*Hab. 2:14 For the earth will be filled with the **knowledge** of the glory of the LORD, as the waters cover the sea.*

Isa. 65:17-18, Isa. 65:23-25 "Behold, I will create new heavens and a new earth. The former things will not be remembered, nor will they come to mind. But be glad and rejoice forever in what I will create, for I will create Jerusalem to be a delight and its people a joy... They will be a people blessed by the LORD, they and their descendants with them. Before they call I will answer; while they are still speaking I will hear. The <u>wolf and the lamb</u> will feed together, and the <u>lion</u> will eat straw like the ox... They will neither harm nor destroy on all my holy mountain," says the LORD."

It is interesting to note that in this new age, on the mountain of Jerusalem, at least, all of the eating being mentioned in this text is non-meat, pretty much like the diet before the Fall, and there is no harming or destroying of anyone, man or animal.

But key is this - the animals already know God to some degree, and they will at some point in the future be abundantly filled with the **knowledge** of God and behave in friendly, loving ways with other species, animal and human. The law will be written on every living being's heart in the peaceable kingdom. How wonderful it will be when we can all relate lovingly with one another, humans and animals together!

Like a Child

We saw earlier how God spared Nineveh, partly for the sakes of the very young children and the animals. The beasts and the children are closer to innocence and wonder, to freely-given love. Puppies and dogs, full of life and enthusiasm, wiggle and fall all over themselves to give you love as much as they can, unconditionally! Their hearts are on their sleeves, and they don't hold back. They accept and give love openly and gladly.

Jesus said that the kingdom of heaven belongs to those like little children. He was talking to and about humans, certainly, but if the kingdom of heaven is for those with the humility and low status of little children, and God loves all His creation as deeply as we have seen, then it would seem that the kingdom of heaven is for the animals too, since they are in some ways similar to little children, and God spared Ninevah partly for little children <u>and the animals</u>.

Matt. 18:3 And (Jesus) said: "I tell you the truth, unless you change and become like <u>little</u> children, you will never enter the kingdom of heaven!"

Matt. 18:14 Your Father in heaven is not willing that any of these <u>little</u> ones should be lost.

Mark 10:13-15 People were bringing little children to Jesus to have Him touch them, but the disciples rebuked them. When Jesus saw this, He was indignant. He said to them, "Let the <u>little</u> children come to Me, and do not hinder them, for the Kingdom of God belongs to such as these. I tell you the truth, anyone who will not receive the Kingdom of God like a <u>little</u> child will never enter it." And He took the children in His arms, put His hands on them and blessed them.

Isa. 40:9-11 You who bring good tidings to Jerusalem, lift up your voice with a shout, lift it up, do not be afraid; say to the towns of Judah, "Here is your God!" See, the Sovereign LORD comes with power, and His arm rules for Him. See, His reward is with Him...He tends His flock like a shepherd: He gathers the lambs in His arms and carries them close to His heart; He gently leads those that have young.

That last one is an analogy, and yet it depicts the Sovereign LORD as gently caring for sheep and lambs, to show how He tends His human flock. God was not above being depicted in this way and in fact does care for His animals too.

▪ Creation Proclaims God's Salvation

As we have seen, the Psalms and other scriptures speak of creation praising God. God is intimately involved in every detail of His creation, knowing every creature, and clothing the land in beauty and magnificence. Not only that, but God will reconcile <u>all</u> creation to Himself. Here is what Paul wrote - note the repeated use of the words "everything" and "all":

> *Col. 1:16-20, Col. 1:23 For by Him all things were created... All things were created by Him and for Him. He is before all things, and <u>in Him all things hold together</u> ... He is the beginning and the firstborn from among the dead, so that <u>in everything</u> He might have the supremacy (some translations: "first place"; "chief place"). For God was pleased to have all His fullness dwell in Him, and through Him to <u>reconcile</u> to Himself <u>all things</u>, whether things on earth or things in heaven, by making peace through His blood, shed on the cross... This is the gospel that you heard and that has been* **proclaimed** <u>to every creature</u> *(some translations: "<u>in all creation</u>") under heaven.*

One can't truly have supremacy or hold first place in "everything" if everything doesn't still exist. It does not stand to reason that God would only save some humans out of His Son's great sacrifice for the world, when <u>all</u> of His wondrous creation that He loves could praise Him and be reconciled to and united with him.

Psalm 6:5 No one remembers You when he is dead. Who praises You from the grave?

Psalm 30:3, Psalm 30:9, Psalm 30:11-12 O LORD, You brought me up from the grave... What gain is there in my destruction...? Will the dust praise You? Will it proclaim Your faithfulness? ...You turned my wailing into dancing; You clothed me with joy, that my heart may sing to You and <u>not be silent</u>. O LORD, my God, I will give You... thanks <u>forever</u>.

It is the *living* who will praise Him, with thanks and joy in our salvation! And the seas will roar, and nature sing...

God, through His Son, reconciles *all* things, holds everything together, and rules His whole creation, not just a fraction of it. In Revelation, the Messiah tells John, *"These are the words of... the ruler of God's <u>creation</u>." (Rev. 3:14)*

Some translations of the *Col. 1:23* passage earlier in this chapter say *"Good News that has been proclaimed <u>to</u> all creation"*, but my research finds that *"proclaimed <u>in</u> all creation"* (like some translations have) is a closer translation of the Greek. The Good News that has been proclaimed <u>in</u> all creation on earth may be that God <u>saves</u> it, He <u>renews</u> it, and He rules it, including mankind <u>and</u> all of His creatures. All creation can see/sense aspects of it, but it is also evidenced <u>in</u> creation itself.

Perhaps one way that the Good News of God's salvation is proclaimed **in** all creation is by showing how life and renewal follow apparent death and decline, in many different examples within creation. In fact, the Jewish calendar is even built on the good, bright thing following the dark thing - a Jewish day starts in the evening with the dark night followed by morning and light, and this is evident in the Bible as well:

Gen. 1:5 And there was evening, and there was morning- the first day.

Labor and stress for six days are followed by rest and peace on the seventh day of each week:

Ex. 23:12 Six days do your work, but on the seventh day do not work, so that your ox and your donkey may rest and the slave born in your household, and the alien as well, may be refreshed.

The Jewish year essentially starts with autumn (the beginning of annual decline/decay), followed by the barrenness and darkness of winter with many trees and plants looking dead, and *then* spring bursts forth with abundant life and flowers and new leaves on trees, followed by the glory of summer with warmth and plentiful fresh foods.

For a baby, the frightening and unpleasant end of life in the womb as he or she knew it (expulsion through labor) is followed by birth into a new world. For a mother, the pain and work of labor are followed by the gift of a child and the youthful renewal of the essence of the parents for a new generation.

Seeds are buried in the ground, to all appearances gone and dead, but then they shoot forth with new life as strong, vibrant plants that are much greater than the seed ever was!

> *1 Cor. 15:36-38 What you sow does not come to life unless it dies. When you sow, you do not plant the body that will be, but just a seed, perhaps of wheat or of something else. But God gives it a body as he has determined, and to each kind of seed he gives its own body.*

Worm-like and gravity-bound caterpillars crawl on a branch and embed themselves in the shroud of a cocoon, to all appearances gone and dead, but then they emerge as some of the most beautiful creatures in all of creation, brilliantly-colored butterflies with the ability to fly in the heavens!

Thus creation repeatedly proclaims the good news of God's salvation and renewal of things that suffered decay and an ending - it was not The End. It gets better, my friends, and the best is still to come!

> *Psalm 96:1-2 Sing to the LORD, <u>all the earth</u>. Sing to the LORD, praise His Name; <u>proclaim His salvation</u> day after day.*

So in all these things creation proclaims that God saves, He is powerful, He renews - and life follows death, thanks to the salvation by God our Creator and creation's reconciliation with Him.

> *Weeping may remain for a night, but rejoicing comes in the morning. (Psalm 30:5)*

Elimination of Death - For All!

Not only does creation illustrate and reinforce the hope of life after death, death itself will be eliminated. It came into the world at the Fall due to man's disobedience, catching all creation up in bondage to it, but, through the Messiah's obedient act of redemption and salvation, death was conquered and shall be eliminated, and **all creation** shall be released from it.

Let's review:

Creation is bound up in the fall <u>and</u> salvation of mankind:

> *Rom. 8:19-21 (Bible in Basic English) For the strong desire of <u>every living thing</u> is waiting for the revelation of the sons of God. For <u>every living thing</u> was put under the power of change, not by its desire, but by him who made it so, in <u>hope</u> that <u>all living things</u> will be <u>made free from the power of death</u> and <u>will have a part</u> with the free children of God <u>in glory</u>.*

The Messiah has control over death and even abolishes death, as stated in these two passages:

Rev. 1:18 I am the Living One; I was dead, and behold I am alive for ever and ever! And I hold the keys of death and Hades.

2 Tim. 1:9-10 This grace was given... before the beginning of time, but it has now been revealed through the appearing of our Savior, Christ Jesus, who has <u>destroyed</u> <u>death</u> and has brought life and immortality to light through the gospel.

So God's plan was before the beginning of time. And the gospel, the Good News, is proclaimed in all creation. Jesus even made the point that those who have died are living:

*Matt. 22:31-32 (Jesus replied,...) "But about the resurrection of the dead - have you not read what God said to you, 'I <u>**am**</u> the God of Abraham, the God of Isaac, and the God of Jacob'? He is not the God of the dead but of the <u>living</u>."* Side note: It is interesting that Jesus said, "what <u>*God said to you*</u>". He affirmed that scripture (at least what existed at that time), is what <u>*God said*</u> to His people, not just something written by humans alone.

Luke 20:38 (Jesus replied,...) "He is not the God of the dead, but of the living, for to Him <u>all are alive</u>."

Scripture before the Messiah's first coming also foretells that death itself will be completely eliminated, that God will provide salvation:

Isa. 25:7-9 On this mountain (the LORD Almighty) will <u>destroy</u> the shroud that enfolds all peoples, the *sheet that covers all nations; <u>He will swallow up death forever</u>. The Sovereign LORD will wipe away the tears from all faces; He will remove the disgrace of His people from all the earth. The LORD has spoken. In that day they will say, "Surely this is our God; we trusted in Him, and He <u>saved</u> us. This is the LORD, we trusted in Him; let us rejoice and be glad in His <u>salvation</u>."*

God wants to save and does save. He does not at all enjoy seeing any of His creation perish, even if by personal choice. Even the human who deliberately rejects Him and persists in doing evil, God wants to turn to Him, to accept Him, and <u>live</u>:

Ezek. 18:23, Ezek. 18:32; Ezek. 33:11 Do I take any pleasure in the death of the wicked? declares the Sovereign LORD. Rather, am I not pleased when they turn from their ways and live?... For I take no pleasure in the death of anyone, declares the Sovereign LORD. Repent and live!... Say to them, "As surely as I live, declares the sovereign LORD, I take no pleasure in the death of the wicked, but rather that they turn from their ways and live. Turn! Turn from your evil ways! Why will you die...?"

God prefers to show mercy. Yes, He (understandably) gets angry at sin and being defied, rejected, or ignored, but He loves mankind and all His creation and means to save them. Consider that He saved some of every kind of animal along with man during the Flood - He didn't just save domestic animals, He saved *every kind* of animal, which surely took some doing!

Micah 7:18-19 Who is a God like You, Who pardons sin and forgives the transgression of the remnant of His inheritance? You do not stay angry forever but delight to show mercy. You will again have compassion on us; You will tread our sins underfoot and hurl all our iniquities into the depths of the sea.

The above verse is depicted as Israel praising God for its coming restoration, but it speaks of Who God is, a God Who pardons sin and <u>delights to show mercy</u> to all who welcome it and gladly receive it.

Psalm 16:9-11 Therefore my heart is glad and my tongue rejoices; my body also will rest secure, because <u>You will not abandon me to the grave</u>... You have made known to me the path of <u>life</u>; You will fill me with joy in Your presence, with <u>eternal</u> pleasures at Your right hand.

And God ultimately destroys death itself and makes everything new:

Rev. 21:4-5 "There will be no more death or mourning or crying or pain, for the old order of things has passed away." He Who was seated on the throne said, "I am making <u>everything</u> new!"

Some things at the end times will be destroyed, death being one of them, and will presumably not be made new (but everything remaining will be made new). In *Revelation chapter 20*, before death is destroyed, the devil is thrown into the lake of burning brimstone. The sea gives up the dead that were in it, and death and Hades give up their dead. Each person (I believe, human) is judged according to what he has done, as recorded in books. Then death and Hades are thrown into the lake of burning brimstone which is the second death, and any person whose name is not found written in the book of life is thrown into the lake of fire also.

What one has done is not only deeds or lack thereof, but also choices one has made. So if one has placed one's trust in God and welcomed God's salvation, those too would be things that one has done that likely would've been recorded. I do not know if that includes choices made after the moment the body dies, when one's spirit meets God. Perhaps that is a possibility, but of course it would be far better to seek and accept God while in this world, in the body! <u>This</u> world is the testing ground for how you choose to live, how much you love and help others, and whether you love and fear God, turning to and calling upon Him for help and guidance.

Isa. 55:3, Isa. 55:6-7 Give ear and come to Me; hear Me, that your soul may live… Seek the LORD while He may be found; call on Him while He is near. Let the wicked forsake his way and the evil man his thoughts. Let him turn to the LORD, and He will have mercy on him, and to our God, for He will freely pardon.

In any case, after the devil, death, Hades, and the persons whose names were not found in the book of life have been thrown into the lake of fire, everything that remains is renewed - ***everything***! (*Rev. 21:5*) Jesus referred to this renewal, when He said: "*I tell you the* *truth, at the <u>renewal of all things</u>, when the Son of Man sits on His glorious throne…" (Matt. 19:28)*

"Everything" and "all things" surely include God's animals who have been carried along with the downs and ups of mankind all along.

> *Isa. 42:10-11 "I am the LORD; that is My Name! I will not give My glory to another or My praise to idols. See, the former things have taken place, and <u>new</u> things I declare; before they spring into being, I announce them to you." Sing to the LORD a new song, His praise from the ends of the earth, you who go down to the sea, and <u>all that is in it</u>, you <u>islands</u>, and all who live in them. Let the <u>desert</u> and its towns raise their voices…*

It is <u>all</u> who are in the sea, <u>all</u> who live in the islands, <u>all</u> those in the desert, even the islands and desert themselves, God's creation, praising Him!

All Rejoice

Throughout scripture, animals are included in exhortations to praise God, as part of His creation praising Him now, and in times to come. All of God's great and beautiful creation sings to Him and breaks out in rejoicing! Why would He have it be any less? Lord, glorify Your name in ***all*** the earth!

The scriptures show that <u>all</u> creation praises and will praise God, including the land and the trees, the mountains and the seas, the heavens and the earth, and

<u>every</u> creature in them - *every creature*. I do not think this is only metaphorical, I think it is *true*. I may not be able to hear all of the ways that creation sings, at least not in this body, but God can. Just think - the music of the spheres! God's creation is more than the earth and all creatures in it - it's the universe, the stars, the angels, and it <u>all</u> praises and will praise God.

God Himself said to Job, *"Where were you when I laid the earth's foundation?... On what were its footings set, or who laid its cornerstone - while the morning stars sang together, and all the angels shouted for joy?" (Job 38:4, Job 38:6-7)* Jesus even said that the stones would shout their praise:

> *Luke 19:37-40 The whole crowd of disciples began joyfully to praise God in loud voices for all the miracles they had seen: "Blessed is the King who comes in the name of the Lord!" "Peace in heaven and glory in the highest!" Some of the Pharisees in the crowd said to Jesus, "Teacher, rebuke your disciples!" "I tell you," He replied, "if they keep quiet, the stones will cry out."*

I hope for and look forward to the day when I hear all creation sing! You don't have to believe these things literally, but it sure is exhilarating if you do, and let yourself be filled with wonder and hope in the greatness and majesty of God and the things He has in store for us.

Psalms 96 and 98 say that nature will rejoice when God comes to judge the earth. Some translations say that nature will rejoice when He is coming to <u>rule</u> the earth:

Psalm 96:11-13 (JPS Tanakh) Let the heavens rejoice and the earth exult; let the sea and all within it thunder, the fields and everything in them exult; then shall all the trees of the forest shout for joy at the presence of the LORD, for He is coming, for He is coming to rule the earth; He will rule the world justly and its peoples in faithfulness.

Perhaps creation welcomes its Creator's arrival because it glorifies Him, He's here, now He will set things right and rule justly, evil will be defeated, and <u>creation will be released from its bondage to death</u>!

All creatures praise God and have reason to praise God. He glorifies His Name in all creation. God saves the world, and His creatures praise and shall praise Him. He made us all, human and animal, and we are His. I close with these scripture selections - praise God, *all* creatures!

Psalm 100:1-3, Psalm 100:5 Shout for joy to the LORD, <u>all the earth</u>. Worship the LORD with gladness; come before Him with joyful songs. Know that the LORD is God. <u>It is He Who made us, and we are His</u>... For the LORD is good and His love endures <u>forever</u>...

Psalm 148:7-13 Praise the LORD from the earth, <u>you great sea creatures</u> and all ocean depths, lightning *and hail, snow and clouds, stormy winds <u>that do His bidding</u>, you mountains and all hills, fruit trees and all cedars, <u>wild animals and all cattle, small creatures and flying birds</u>, kings of the earth and all nations, nations, ... young and maidens, old men and children. Let them praise the name of the LORD...*

Isa. 44:23 Sing for joy, O heavens, for the LORD has done this; shout aloud, O earth beneath. Burst into song, you mountains, you forests and all your trees...

Isa. 55:12-13 You will go out in joy and be led forth in peace; the mountains and hills will burst into song before you, and all the trees of the field will clap their hands. Instead of the thornbush will grow the pine tree, and instead of briers the myrtle will grow. This will be <u>for the LORD's renown</u>, for an <u>everlasting</u> sign which will not be destroyed.

Psalm 66:1-2, Psalm 66:4 Shout with joy to God, <u>all the earth</u>! Sing the glory of His Name; make His praise glorious!... <u>All the earth</u> bows down to You; they sing praise to You, they sing praise to Your Name.

Psalm 69:35 Let heaven and earth praise Him, the seas and <u>all that move in them</u>.

*Rev. 5:13-14 Then I heard **every creature** in heaven and on earth and under the earth and on the sea, and all that is in them, <u>singing</u>, "To Him who sits on the throne and to the Lamb be praise and honor and glory and power, for ever and ever!" The four living creatures said, "Amen"...*

Let everything that has breath praise the LORD.

(Psalm 150:6)

Index